Write It

Teacher's Book

Write It

Writing skills for intermediate learners of English

Teacher's Book

Michael Dean

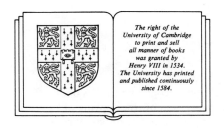

The right of the
University of Cambridge
to print and sell
all manner of books
was granted by
Henry VIII in 1534.
The University has printed
and published continuously
since 1584.

Cambridge University Press
Cambridge
New York   New Rochelle
Melbourne   Sydney

Published by the Press Syndicate of the University of Cambridge
The Pitt Building, Trumpington Street, Cambridge CB2 1RP
35 East 57th Street, New York, NY 10022, USA
10 Stamford Road, Oakleigh, Melbourne 3166, Australia

© Cambridge University Press 1988

First published 1988

Printed in Great Britain
by Bell & Bain Ltd, Glasgow

ISBN 0 521 31172 1 Teacher's Book
ISBN 0 521 31171 3 Learner's Book
ISBN 0 521 32356 8 Cassette

CE

CONTENTS

THANKS

I would like to thank all the schools and teachers who took part in the piloting of this book, especially Eurocentre Lee Green, Sociedade Brasileira de Cultura Inglesa in São Paulo and the Teach-In Language and Training Workshop in Rome.

Thanks to Peter Taylor for the cassette production.

The section on error correction in the Introduction to the teacher was read and commented on by several editors at CUP, by two of my colleagues at Colchester Institute, Tony Kidd and Steve Slater, and by Catherine Walter. I appreciate their time and trouble.

And to Peter Donovan, Margherita Baker, Alison Silver and Angela Wilde at CUP, thanks for the freedom and the support (I needed both).

Michael Dean
Colchester 1988

INTRODUCTION

Scope and dimensions of the book

Level
This is a twenty unit intermediate writing skills book. It is suitable for learners who have had from 150 class hours of English to intermediate learners with five or six years of English.

Gradation
There is a gradation of difficulty from Unit 1 to Unit 20 which accommodates the span of learner ability indicated above.

Length of units
The twenty units in the Learner's Book average two or three class hours each, depending on how much of the writing is done in class. Sometimes additional tasks are suggested in the Teacher's Book and if these are introduced more time must be allowed. In the longer units some exercises are marked with an asterisk (*). These can be omitted if there is time pressure, or done as homework.

Order of units
The units are independent of each other, so it is possible to leave some units out and do others more intensively, developing all the ideas in the Teacher's Book and in this Introduction. It is also possible to vary the order of units.

Suggested teaching techniques

The transfer from oral / aural to written work
Although the traditional text is one stimulus to written work, there are several others and oral/aural work in pairs or groups or as a full class is one of them. These activities require the learners to perform a task orally/aurally first, the teacher adds input, then the learners perform the task in writing.

The stages from oral/aural to written work are as follows:
1 Learners carry out the oral/aural task in the exercise.
2 Teacher monitors language using a Feedback Sheet.
An example of a Feedback Sheet is on the next page.

You said	You should have said	This was interesting

Write learner errors in the *You said* column. Write correct utterances and anything useful the learners could have said but did not in the *This was interesting* column. If the oral/aural work is done as a full class, learners will soon get used to you writing on a Feedback Sheet while they speak (especially if the feedback is mainly positive). If the oral/aural work is done in pairs or small groups they will soon get used to you going round jotting items down.

3 When the oral/aural work is finished you and the learners together correct errors and they write the correct version in the *You should have said* column. Ideally, photocopy the Feedback Sheet for the learners immediately, but you could copy the Feedback Sheet on to the board or an OHP.

4 You and the learners then plan the writing task set in the exercise. You can do this at three levels of support:

Level 1 You and the class do the writing task orally and you write it on the board. You draw the learners' attention to features of language they were getting wrong in the oral/aural phase. When your board writing is complete you cloze it (make gaps by deleting every fifth or seventh word). The better the learners the more gaps you leave. They then write the paragraph, filling in the gaps you left. This considerable degree of support is useful for weak classes writing not more than one paragraph.

Level 2 You and the learners do the writing task orally and you make notes on the board. You write key items of vocabulary and suggest link words like 'however', 'so', 'but'.

Level 3 You write only key vocabulary items on the board.

Notemaking

Notemaking is learners making notes on their own views and experiences (as opposed to notetaking which is from an exterior source like a text or cassette). Learners can make notes before they begin any piece of writing.

However, notemaking really comes into its own when learners are writing two or three paragraphs or more. Learners then make notes before they start writing and hand the notes in as a Writing Plan. The teacher then corrects aspects like the logical ordering of material, paragraphing and linking between paragraphs before learners start to write. This leaves the teacher free to concentrate on sentence level language errors when the writing is handed in.

Error correction

Here are some suggestions for correcting written work:

1 Correct the errors in the written work and give the work back to the learners. Ask if they have any questions about your corrections. Possibly ask them to rewrite incorrect sentences correctly.

2 Go round correcting learners' work in class as they are writing.

3 Underline the errors on learners' written work but do not correct them. Draw up a Feedback Sheet. A Feedback Sheet for learners' written errors looks like this:

You wrote	You should have written	Why
I have told him yesterday	*I told him yesterday*	*Tense*

Copy a representative sample of learners' errors (not all of them) on to the *You wrote* column of the Feedback Sheet. Photocopy the Feedback Sheet so each learner has a copy. In class, you and the learners correct the errors and the learners write the correction in the *You should have written* column. You and the learners classify each of the errors in the *Why* column. For example, the error might be Tense, Preposition, Subject–Verb agreement and so on. You will need a 'miscellaneous' category like Wrong Phrase to cover semantic errors.

When you have used this kind of Feedback Sheet three or four times you and the learners together decide which error categories are coming up most often. You and the learners might like to decide together on a numbering system for the error categories. For example, Tense could be 1, Articles could be 2, Wrong Phrase could be 3, and so on. Do not have more than nine categories, including the miscellaneous 'catch all' category of Wrong Phrase.

Next time you use a Feedback Sheet for written errors use the numbering system that you and the learners devised.

Learners should correct the errors you underlined on their own written work as well as correcting the errors on the Feedback Sheet. However, instead of learners correcting after each homework you could have a correction session in class, after, say, three homeworks. At the correction session learners correct the errors you underlined with reference to the Feedback Sheets that you and they filled in. Learners could also put the error number in the margin, using the numbering system you and the learners have devised.

4 Underline the errors in the learners' work *or* write the number of errors the learner made at the bottom of the page.

In class, learners in small groups correct the errors in pencil. Take the work in again and check the corrections. This technique works best for short pieces of work, of paragraph length or less. It is particularly useful in mixed ability groups.

5 This is a variant of 4 (above). Underline the errors in the learners' work *or* write the number of errors the learner made at the bottom of the page.

In class, learners in small groups correct the errors in pencil. Each small group is responsible for one type of error only (for example, Tense or Preposition or Wrong Phrase). Learners' work is passed from group to group, so as many types of error as possible are looked for and corrected.

6 Learners in pairs correct each other's work before you have seen it. They can correct each other after every paragraph or after they have finished writing. Then take the work in and correct both the work and the learners' corrections.

7 When learners have finished writing in class, a learner, or two or three learners, copy their writing on to the board and you and the class correct it, sentence by sentence. This is clearly for work of paragraph length or less.

In my opinion all these correction techniques should be used, but 3, which is the most thorough, is time consuming and can only be used occasionally.

Upgrading

Upgrading is helping the learners to rewrite their work at a level more like a native speaker. This important technique not only raises the level of learners' English but helps them to develop an intuition, a 'feel', for the language.

Upgrading is concerned not with language error but with grammatically correct language that would not sound natural to a native speaker. It is concerned with features like over-simple language, incorrect selection of material, incorrect prioritization of information and viewpoint, incorrect thematization (making the wrong thing the subject of the sentence), failure to state or restate the subject of a sentence, misunderstanding the social implications of language (for example 'I want' instead of 'I would like'), misusing idiom or using idiom too little or too much, and incorrect or fluctuating register (too formal or too informal).

Only some of these categories can be made overt to intermediate learners. However, learners should be told to watch out for language that is rude or over-polite, too formal or too informal and too simple. The word 'unnatural' will have to cover the other categories above.

Steps in upgrading are as follows:

1 Make it clear to the learners that they will be asked to rewrite work produced by a different member of the class from time to time. This is an inevitable part of raising the level of their English and does not mean the work was unsatisfactory. Ideally, each learner in the class should have his or her work upgraded once during the year.

2 Put a corrected piece of written work on an OHP (the board will do) and ask for further improvements. You will have to do nearly all of the upgrading yourself. So upgrade the work, sentence by sentence, until it is at or nearer native-speaker level. Let one or two learners read it aloud to get the feel of it. Then they copy it down, preferably with a time limit.

3 Learners keep upgraded work as a model and ideally should refer to it from time to time.

Another way of upgrading is to work with the learners while they are writing in class.

Recycling

Recycling is using the learners' own work as a stimulus to further writing. Learners read the corrected version of another learner's letter, for example, and then reply to it.

If you are doing one of the units intensively there is plenty of opportunity for recycling, especially among the personal letters.

Symbols

= Cassette

* = The exercise can be omitted or done as homework.

SECTION 1: BRIEF PERSONAL WRITING

1 FILLING IN PERSONAL FORMS

—— **1** ————————————————————————
Aims

1 Revision of learners' personal data in English.
2 Relating form filling to the learners' own world.

Teacher input

1 The alphabet in English.
2 Hobbies as a word field.

Procedure

1 Revise the alphabet in English.
2 Elicit learners' hobbies and list them on the board.

——**2** 📼 ————————————————————————
Aim

Understanding and filling in grids with printed and oral input.

Teacher input

Pre-teaching: Ask learners to list ways in which an unemployed person could keep busy. Teach 'play squash' and 'go to a multigym' to start them off.

Procedure

1 Check comprehension of the leaflet before you play the cassette.
2 Learners fill in the Timeplan from the cassette and the leaflet.
3 Discuss answers with learners using the Key to answers which follows.
4* Learners imagine that Tim is writing to a friend about the Timeplan, and write sentences on this pattern. Put the pattern on the board.
   On (DAY) I go to (PLACE) at (TIME) and I (ACTIVITY) – with (PERSON). It only costs me (PRICE).

1

Answers

Tim's Timeplan for one week in March

Day	Time	Activity	Place	Cost
Monday	8–9 pm	gym	Leytonstone	50p
Tuesday	5–6 pm	tennis	War Memorial Park	35p
Wednesday	lunchtime	squash	Leytonstone	70p
Thursday				
Friday	8–9 pm	gym	Leytonstone	50p
Saturday	2.30–3.30	waterfun	Waltham Forest	45p
Sunday	morning	swimming	Waltham Forest	30p
			Total cost per week	£2.80

Key to answers (especially Saturday and Sunday)

1 Saturday: Joanna says waterfun is in the same pool as the swimming, which means Waltham Forest. Waterfun at Waltham Forest is from 2.30 to 3.30 pm.
2 Sunday: Tim says he is not going swimming at Leytonstone, and Leyton is not open on Sunday morning, which leaves Waltham Forest.
3 All other information is stated on the cassette directly or is in the leaflet.

2 WRITING GREETINGS CARDS

——— **1** ———————————————————————

Aim

To establish what learners already know in this area and to use better learners' performance to help weaker learners.

Teacher input

1 In 1.1 teach useful prepositions and adverbial particles. For example 'to send *to*', '*at* Christmas', '*on* his birthday'. If you have time, mention constructions like 'I sent *them* a card when they got married.'
2 In 1.2 help learners write specific greetings as required.

Procedure

After 1.2 write learners' greetings on the board for the class to copy down, if necessary. Add any greetings that you have written recently yourself.

Note Learners might be interested in the following: according to the Greeting Card and Calendar Association about 1,900 million greetings cards are sent in Britain every year. This includes not only Christmas, birthdays and ordinary wedding anniversaries but also Silver Wedding anniversaries (25 years), Ruby (40 years), Golden (50) and Diamond (usually 60 but sometimes 75 as well). Cards are also sent on Mother's Day (the fourth Sunday in Lent, usually in March) and Father's Day (the third Sunday in June). You could also mention Valentine's Day cards at this point. Learners are asked to write a Valentine in Exercise 3.

>>>→

--- **2** ---

Aim

Information transfer of idiomatic written greetings. This exercise is the input to the writing in Exercise 3.

Answers

1 c, g, l	5 g, m
2 e, j	6 i, k
3 a, d, l	7 b, g
4 f, h	

Note   The situation in (d) is that someone was helped to move house by friends. This situation is used in the cassette exercise in Unit 8.

--- **3** ---

Aim

Writing greetings using some of the information from Exercise 2.

Teacher input

This is to be done as a full class. Go round, helping learners as they write, correcting errors and providing vocabulary where needed.

3 WRITING POSTCARDS

1

Aims

1 To get the learners used to a 'postcard style' of writing by contrasting it with other styles.
2 To provide input for Exercise 2.

Answers

1.1 b, d, e, g, h, i, j are from a postcard.
1.2 a) Last year   c) ... we shall land ... at 1500 hours   f) This is urgent!

2

Aim

Guided writing for the learners to construct a model postcard for themselves.

Procedure

Method 1   Ask all learners to write the postcard, not just identify the correct letters in Exercise 1. *OR*

Method 2   The first person in each pair closes the book. The second person dictates the postcard, in the correct order, from the sentences in Exercise 1.

Answers

(i, j, g, h, d, b, e)   Dear John, We are in the Algarve for two weeks. From our villa you can see right out over the bay and the little town of Albufeira in the distance; it's beautiful. The local village consists of three houses, a grocery shop and four bars! Jean has just climbed out of the swimming pool and I'm just sitting here, looking at the almond blossom. It's paradise here, I'm not coming back! Lots of love, Jean and Phyllis

—— **3** ——————————————————————

Aims

1 Guided postcard writing.
2 Order of sentences.
3 Word order within sentences.

Teacher input

Here is a guideline for word order within sentences: S, V, O, P, T (Subject, Verb, Object, Place, Time). The order can sometimes be varied, for example, sentence (e) could be 'Tomorrow we're going on a trip to Prague' as well as 'We're going on a trip to Prague tomorrow'. But S, V, O, P, T is the usual word order in English.

Procedure

After the learners have done the exercise, write each sentence of the postcard on the board asking the learners to identify S, V, O, P, T as you write. Point out the sentence (e) variant above. (It applies to all Time words and phrases.)

Answer

(b, f, c, a, e, d, g)   Dear Susie, Well, here we are in Czechoslovakia! It's a really nice country. We're in a beautiful, unspoilt place. In fact our little hotel is miles from anywhere. We're going on a trip to Prague tomorrow. We're really looking forward to it. Love to everyone in the office, Roger

—— **4** ——————————————————————

Aims

1 Teaching a possible framework for postcards.
2 Order of sentences.
3 Relating postcard writing to the learners' world.

Procedure

4.2 could be homework. Alternatively, check learners' writing as they write in class.

Answers to 4.1

a) our   b) hotel   c) At the moment   d) It's nice here

Note   There is more on describing the learners' town in Unit 15.

---5 --------------------------------

Aim

Free writing within a loose framework.

Teacher input

The learners will need your help. Two frameworks follow. The framework 'Enjoyment on holiday' gives further phrases for having a nice time. They are in increasing order of strength from column 1 to column 3. The second framework is a different 'Model for postcard writing'; this one uses the simple past tense.

Procedure

1 Put some or all of the 'Enjoyment on holiday' framework on the board or OHP before you play the cassette. Learners may be able to suggest more phrases of their own.
2 Put the 'Model for postcard writing' on the board or OHP before you play the cassette. Ask learners to take notes from the cassette using the 'Model' as a framework.
3 Play the cassette as many times as the learners want to hear it. Learners take notes.

Method 1   Learners write a postcard or postcards for homework, using the notes they took in class. *OR*

Method 2   All learners take notes on all three postcards. Learners write the postcards in class in pairs or small groups. You go round the class helping. *OR*

Method 3   Learners are divided into three groups. All learners listen to all three postcards but Group 1 takes notes on Postcard 1 only, Group 2 on Postcard 2 and Group 3 on Postcard 3. Learners write the postcards in class with your help and read them to other groups. Replay the relevant 'Postcard' on the cassette before each reading.

Section 1: Brief personal forms

ENJOYMENT ON HOLIDAY

	1	2	3
Subjective	We're enjoying ourselves here.	We're having a really great time here.	This is the best holiday I've ever had.
	I feel rested here.	I feel really tranquil here.	I feel completely at peace here.
	I feel good.	I feel great.	I feel fantastic!
	I'm happy here.	I'm very happy here.	I am blissfully happy here!
	I'm having a good time.	I'm having a great time.	I'm having the time of my life!
Objective	It's interesting here.	It's really very interesting here.	It's fascinating here.
	This is an attractive city.	It's a beautiful city.	It's the most beautiful city I've ever seen.
	The scenery is very pleasant.	The scenery is spectacular.	The scenery is absolutely breathtaking.

MODEL FOR POSTCARD WRITING

1 Greeting (optional).

2 What I did yesterday or last week.

3 Description of the place.

4 Best wishes, regards, greetings to someone back home.

SECTION 2: LONGER PERSONAL WRITING

4 WRITING NOTES

—— **1** ————————————————————————————

Aim

1 Presenting a possible framework for notes.

Teacher input

Work on the present perfect tense. A note is often about a past event which has implications for the present and the future; so the present perfect is often used. Revise the present perfect with the class before starting Exercise 1. It might be helpful to use Note C in Exercise 1 as an illustration of the present perfect.

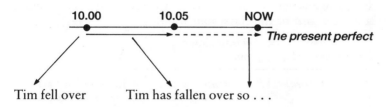

PAST TIME   **FUTURE TIME**

10.00   10.05   NOW

The present perfect

Tim fell over   Tim has fallen over so . . .

Note The time/tense diagram above explains the particular present perfect sentences in the exercise. However, it is also possible to see the present perfect as a 'retrospective' tense, looking back at a past event from NOW rather than forward through NOW to the future, as shown in the diagram.

Procedure

Learners use 1.1 to practise the present perfect and write the opening sentences of notes. Elicit and check the answers. Point out that the sentences in 1.2 follow on from the opening sentence in 1.1, making three sentences for each pair of pictures.

9

Suggested answers

1.1 A Peter, Roger's just phoned from the station.
    B Sue, Bill's car has broken down.
    C Darling, Tim's fallen over.
    D Anne, we've decided to go to the café on the corner.
1.2 A He's brought Ethel with him. I've gone to pick them up.
    B I've given him a lift into town. I'll be back later.
    C He's cut his knee. I've taken him to hospital.
    D Come and join us if you want to. Jill and Caroline.

―― **2** ――――――――――――――――――――――――

Aim

Practising the structure for notes taught in Exercise 1.

Teacher input

Pre-teach 'spots', 'temperature', 'in tears', 'walked out', 'a row', and 'change of plan'.

Possible answers

(But accept any answer that makes sense. Corrected answers could be pinned on the board or the classroom wall.)

	What has happened	The situation or problem	Action
A	*The TV won't work.*	The picture's got stripes on it.	I've taken it back to the shop. Back soon.
B	*Tom's not feeling very well.*	He's got spots on his face and a high temperature.	*I've taken him to the doctor.*
C	Sandra's just phoned. She's in tears.	*A friend of hers has been killed in an accident.*	*I've gone over to see if I can help in any way.*
D	*Fred's very upset.*	His wife has walked out on him.	*I'm taking him out for a drink.*
E	*Tim's record player won't work.*	*He says he needs it urgently, for a party I think.*	So I've gone over to mend it for him.

What has happened	The situation or problem	Action
F *Bill's father was on the phone.*	Bill got jealous, had a row with Sarah, and left the house.	*Can you phone Bill's father back and tell him where Bill is (if you know)?*
G There's been a change of plan.	*We're meeting at my house instead of at the disco.*	See you there then?
H *I've just got the results at last.*	I've passed all my exams!	*Can you come over and celebrate with me?*
I You'll never guess what's happened!	*Annette has had a sex change operation.*	*She's now called Alan.*

----- **3** -----

Aims

1 Punctuation.
2 Linking.

Teacher input

Here are some punctuation guidelines. There is a longer exercise on punctuation in Unit 11. Some of the information below could be introduced then.

i)   *Question marks:* Used for questions and tentative suggestions.

ii)   *Capital letters:* Capital letters for 'Dear Sir/Madam' and for 'Yours' but not for 'faithfully' or 'sincerely.'

Capital letters for all names, so 'Bristol University' but not 'I went to university', and for 'Leigh Woods' but not 'We went to the woods.'

Capital letters for the first word of each sentence and for abbreviations like RAF (Royal Air Force).

Languages and nationalities have a capital letter even when used as an adjective, like 'French cheese.'

'I' has a capital letter.

iii)   *Full stops:* Full stops at the end of each sentence.

Full stops after abbreviations like, 'etc.' and 'e.g.'

No full stop where the abbreviation reads like a word as in NATO.

iv) *Commas:* There is a comprehensive description of comma usage in *Practical English Usage* (Swan, Oxford University Press) section 506. Swan gives these two examples:

Example 1: Mrs Grange, who was sitting behind the reception desk, gave me a big smile (non-identifying relative clause).

Example 2: If you're ever in London, come and look me up (following adverbial clause).

Here are two short cuts for intermediate learners:

Short cut 1: Put commas in long sentences only where you would need to breathe if you were saying it.

Short cut 2: If in doubt, leave it out.

v) *Apostrophes:* Apostrophes are used in contracted forms like 'can't' and 'don't' where a letter has been omitted.

Apostrophes are also used in genitive forms indicating possession, like 'Peter's book'.

vi) *Exclamation marks:* Exclamation marks are often used when something is surprising, especially interesting or funny. For example 'I've got a car!' meaning he has only just thought of this, obvious though it is. (See Unit 11, exercise 4.)

vii) *Inverted commas:* Inverted commas indicate speech or quotation.

They can also replace the phrase 'so-called'. For example, 'the conference' could be used ironically to indicate that it was not a proper conference for some reason.

viii) *Paragraphs:* A paragraph is supposed to indicate a change of subject. In practice, learners should look for a possible new paragraph every six or seven lines.

Each new paragraph should be indented, i.e. it should start about one centimetre in from the left-hand margin, or directly under the end of the greeting in a letter.

Possible answer

(Accept any answer that makes sense.)

Ted and Alice, We've waited for you for half an hour, *but as* you haven't turned up we've decided to go on to the cinema. You can *still* come if you like. It doesn't start until 7.30. *Or* give one of us a ring tomorrow. Hope you are *both* OK. Bob and Carol   7pm

——— 4* ———————————————————————

Aim

Change of plan notes (minimal support).

Teacher input

1 We still want notes of three or four sentences in length from the learners.
2 Here is a possible framework:
   i)   Statement of change of plan.
   ii) Excuse or reason.
   iii) Alternative arrangement.

Procedure

1 Put the above framework on the board.
2 Practise the framework with the learners orally using situation A (John and Cindy).
3 Learners write all three notes (A, B, C).
4* In pairs learners correct each other's notes.
5* Recycling (see Introduction). Learners reply to each other's notes.

Possible answers

A John and Cindy, We'll be a bit late tonight, I'm afraid. Something's come up at the office and I've got to work late. See you around 8.30. Doris
B Mr Williams, I came to start work on the front room at 9.00 as we agreed, but you were out. Please phone me to arrange another time. Bert Morris
C Joan, Sorry, I've got a crisis on my hands. A friend of mine's husband has walked out on her, and I'm visiting her. I'll be back about 6.15. Love, X

—— 5 ——————————————————————————

Aim

Writing notes, cassette input.

Suggested answers

Note 1 (from seven): We can make clothes. We can pay the women to bring cloth in and use wooden needles to sew/make suits. We could sew in our beds at night (so the cameras and the guards can't see us).
Note 2 (from nine): We can make passports from writing paper and cardboard boxes. The guards will give us the ink. We can tell them we want it for the art class.
Note 3 (from twenty-one): We can make a gun out of wood. We can carve it with one of the bread knives.

5 WRITING LETTERS

──── 1 ────────────────────────────

Aims

1 To provide a model as support for the learners' letter in Exercise 5.
2 Register in letters (e.g. the difference in formality between a letter signed James Godwin, and a letter signed James or Mr Godwin).

Teacher input

The more difficult vocabulary items like 'anorak' and 'sleeping bag' recur in the exercises which follow.

Answers to 1.1 and 1.2

1 T (Margaret and I)
2 T (Maria certainly enjoyed her time with us last year)
3 U (... it gets rather cold here in the autumn)
4 F (James Godwin)

──── 2 ────────────────────────────

Aims

1 Vocabulary.
2 Contextualization of listed items.

Teacher input

1 Nationalities (Italian) and the fact that they have a capital letter (revised from Unit 4).
2 The grammar structures are the imperative, positive and negative ('Please bring...' and 'Don't forget to bring...') and the 'will' form for future time reference ('You'll need...').

Procedure

2.1 must be done as a full class as the learners will need your help.

Answers to 2.1

A sleeping bag, an adaptor, warm clothes, a warm coat, an anorak, some Italian cheese, traveller's cheques, a bottle of Italian wine.

— **3** ———————————————————

Aims

1 Practising vocabulary items which it is not necessary to bring.
2 Relating the situation to the learners' world.

Teacher input

1 'Need' + infinitive.
2 Negative of the 'will' form.
3 Vocabulary relevant to the learners' situation, e.g. visas, car documents, injections, formal clothes, clothes for warm countries.

Procedure

This is best done as a full class, with you eliciting items, and providing vocabulary items and writing them on the board within the patterns suggested, for learners to copy down.

— **4** ———————————————————

Aims

1 Vocabulary for food (list).
2 Describing food.

Teacher input

1 Food vocabulary where necessary (4.1).
2 Vocabulary for comparing food and for taste (4.2). For example, 'sweet', 'sour', 'salty', 'sharp', 'good', 'delicious'.

Procedure

The food vocabulary in 4.1 is best introduced in answer to learners' questions while they are working in pairs. The vocabulary for comparing food and taste in 4.2 should be pre-taught, before the exercise itself. The writing in 4.3 could be homework.

——— 5 ———

Aim

Consolidation of what has been learned in the unit.

Teacher input

1 Point out features of letter layout, relating them to the letter in Exercise 1:
   i) Sender's address is on the right.
   ii) The date is under the address.
   iii) 'Dear' has a capital letter.
   iv) 'Dear' plus name is followed by a comma.
   v) Handwritten letters begin under the comma, not against the left-hand margin.
   vi) The ending should also be directly under the comma in (iv).
2 As they are writing to a friend, learners may need endings other than 'Yours sincerely'. In decreasing order of formality other letter endings are Yours, Best wishes, Love, and Love and kisses.

Note There is more on letter layout in Unit 11 (Teacher's Book).

6 LETTERS OF INVITATION, ACCEPTANCE AND REFUSAL

Note There is a storyline running through Units 6 and 7. These units do, however, stand independently.

——— 1 ———

Aims

1 To show learners formal and informal registers applied to invitations, and to show that language varies according to the relationship between addresser and addressee.
2 Input to the writing in 2.2.

Answers

a) friend or girlfriend, informal
b) friend, informal
c) friend, formal
d) friend or girlfriend, informal
e) no relationship, formal
f) colleagues, informal

——— 2 ———

Aims

1 Teaching formal and informal phrases for accepting and declining invitations.
2 Using the language learned in Exercise 1 and 2.1 in writing applied to the learners' own world.

Procedure

2.1 Elicit genuine invitation situations from the class that are of interest to them. You need one formal invitation situation and one informal. As a full class, the learners, with your help, relate the phrases to their situations and complete each phrase.
2.2 At least some of this should be done in class with you checking learners' work as they write. A good exercise for upgrading (see Introduction).

—— 3 ——

Aims

1 Recycling learners' written work.
2 Free writing.

Procedure

This is a recycling exercise (see Introduction). Each learner is given two invitations written by other learners in 2.2. The work from 2.2 could be corrected or you could underline errors and leave them uncorrected. If errors are uncorrected, the learner receiving the invitation in Exercise 3 has to correct it first and then reply to it in writing. One reply should be accepting an invitation, the reply to the other invitation should be a refusal.

7 ARRANGEMENTS IN WRITING

——— 1 ———

Aim

Introducing phrases for making arrangements.

Teacher input

1 The main prepositions for time and place. For example, 'at eight o'clock', 'at the cinema', 'outside the disco', 'at the moment', 'at my house'.
2 I'd like to + infinitive. For example, 'I'd like to go to London.' This is best left as a sentence pattern at this stage rather than as part of the conditional.
3 Two different ways of expressing future time:
We're meeting at ...
I'll meet you at ...

Procedure

1 Practise the prepositions for time and place and the two ways of expressing future time (Teacher input above) by eliciting suggestions from the learners, and getting them to complete the *Making suggestions* column in 1.1 as a full class.
2 Learners do 1.1 in pairs.
3 As pre-teaching for 1.2 ask the learners to imagine they are leaving notes for a friend. The arrangements have been made, so they should use the present progressive form for future time only. Introduce more verbs: 'We're going to see', 'we're playing', 'we're visiting', and so on. Introduce phrases like 'Would you like to come?', 'Would you like to join us?', 'Are you interested (in coming)?' Remind learners to include time and place when they write the five sentences for 1.2.

——— 2 ———

Aims

1 Writing invitations, making arrangements and excuses.
2 Input to Exercises 3 and 4.

Procedure

As an alternative to the procedure in the Learner's Book, 2.3 can be done as a dictation like this:

After completing 2.2 learners close their books. From Telephone conversation 1 you dictate 'Alan:' then a nominated learner dictates from memory 'Hello, Chantal. This is Alan.' You dictate 'Chantal: Oh hi, Alan. I was just washing my hair.'

In other words, the telephone conversation is dictated in the order it is printed, with learners dictating any part with gaps and you dictating the rest.

Note It is important for the narrative to do both telephone conversations.

Answer

2.1 Chantal is a friend of Alan and of Frank.

Telephone conversation 1
Alan: Hello, Chantal. This is Alan.
Chantal: Oh hi, Alan. I was just washing my hair.
Alan: I was wondering if you'd like to go to the cinema this evening?
Chantal: The cinema? Oh Alan, I'm afraid I can't. I've made arrangements to go out / I'm going out already.
Alan: Who with?
Chantal: Excuse me, Alan, but I think it's my business who I'm going with. You treat me as if I belong to you sometimes. Alan! Alan! He's rung off. Stupid boy.

Telephone conversation 2
Chantal: Hello, Frank? Chantal. Frank, I don't want to go to the cinema this evening. I want to go somewhere else.
Frank: Why? / What's happened? / Is something wrong?
Chantal: Well, I've just realized I've already seen the film.
Frank: Do you fancy going to Brights instead? / How about Brights?
Chantal: Brights? The nightclub? Yes, that would be lovely / that's a good idea.
Frank: I'll pick you up in fifteen minutes then.
Chantal: Oh, we're going by car? OK, lovely.
Frank: I love you.
Chantal: Yes, I love you too. Bye-bye, darling.

—— 3 ————————————————————

Aim

Writing arrangements as events.

Teacher input

The basic tense for narrative of past events is the simple past. Revise it as required.

Procedure

After 3.1 the answers can be written on the board with some words left out (gapped) if the learners need help. Learners fill in the gaps. In 3.2 learners write a letter about four of the things that Frank and Chantal did together. The four things need linking (And then . . .) into one paragraph.

Answers to 3.1

1 Frank and Alan went for a drink after the school reunion.
2 Alan, Chantal and a group of people went to a club after the disco.
3 Alan and Chantal went to a steak bar.
4 Alan and Chantal took a bus to some of the villages near Northampton.
5 Alan and Chantal went for a day trip round Alan's Cambridge college.
6 Frank and Chantal went to Brights nightclub.
7 Frank and Chantal cooked food together for a picnic.
8 Chantal watched Frank play football every week.
9 Frank and Chantal went for long drives, as far as Coventry once, to see the cathedral.
10 Frank and Chantal walked along the river and talked.
11 Chantal asked Frank and Alan to her party.

—— 4 ————————————————————————

Aim

Invitations and arrangements in letters.

Suggested answers

4.1 Letter from Chantal to Frank.

> Darling Frank,
>   Thank you so much for your letter. It was great to hear

about all my friends in Northampton again. The party was wonderful for me too!

Can you come and stay with me in France? It would be marvellous if you could come for Christmas. I know my family would like to meet you. I've told them so much about you.

We could go on a boat trip on the Seine (yes, even in December!). Frank, we could go to the art galleries and I know some nice restaurants and bars. Let me know if you can come.

Love,

Chantal   xx

4.2* Letter from Alan to Chantal.

Dear Chantal,

I was thrilled to get your letter. Yes, I'd love to come and spend Christmas with you and your family.

The boat trip on the Seine sounds great fun and I've always wanted to go to the Louvre and the other art galleries. Paris with you as my guide! I'm really looking forward to it.

I've already booked the ticket. I could make my way to St Denis, I suppose, but could you meet me at Paris Nord? It would be easier.

Looking forward to seeing you.

Love,

Alan

8 LETTERS OF THANKS

──── **1** ────────────────────────────────

Aims

1 Identifying phrases for use in letters of thanks.
2 Writing phrases for use in letters of thanks.

Procedure

1 In 1.1 learners identify which phrases cannot be used in a letter of thanks.
2 After 1.1 you put the reasons why the phrases cannot be used on the board. The reasons are:
   i)   Words too simple.
   ii) Too weak.
   iii) Not for the writer to say.
3 Learners in pairs then work out which wrong phrases are wrong for which reason (see Answers to 1.1 below).
4 In 1.2 learners in pairs try to write a better version of the wrong phrases. Then you help them and they write down your input.

Answers to 1.1

1.1 You can't use c, d, f, h, i, k, m in a letter of thanks. Words too simple (d), too weak (c, h, i, m), not for the writer to say (f, k).

Possible answers to 1.2

c) You have a really lovely house.
d) Thank you for putting us up.
f) We are telling everyone what a great time we had.
h) As usual, we had a marvellous time in Scotland.
i) We enjoyed the meal in the restaurant in Edinburgh.
k) Bob and Tina have got a nice house, although yours is even nicer.
m) Aren't your children smashing?

―――― **2** ――――――――――――――――――――――――

Aim

Vocabulary building (information transfer of thanking phrases).

Teacher input

After the matching in Exercise 2 it might be useful for you and the learners to list words and phrases expressing enthusiasm, praise or appreciation from Exercises 1 and 2.

Answers

1 B
2 C, D
3 A
4 D
5 B
6 A
7 D
8 C
9 A
10 B

―――― **3** ――――――――――――――――――――――――

Aim

Generating thanking phrases related to the learners' own world.

Teacher input

Do the exercise yourself. Elicit and correct learners' answers and write them on the board. Then write up or dictate your own phrases for (a), (b), (c) and (d) that are above intermediate level English. For example:
(a) Thanks so much for lending me that drill and getting me out of a jam.
(b) This came right out of the blue but I'm really pleased.   (c) I had no idea what you were hatching / cooking up for me.   (d) Thanks for working out what the instructions meant.

――――**4** * ――――――――――――――――――――――――

Aim

To present a model letter of thanks with variants.

Teacher input

After the pairwork has been completed and the learners have rewritten the letter, you and the learners change relevant parts of the letter to make other alternatives fit in. For example (j) will fit into the letter if the second sentence is changed to 'It was a good idea to choose...' or 'It was a good idea of yours to choose...'

Answer

Dear Tim,

      I'm writing / This is just to say *thanks a lot / many thanks* for the food you sent from Germany. It was *ever so kind* of you to choose things that we can't get easily here. *I can always use* the dried mushrooms for cooking and we've *begun to eat* the German biscuits already!

      John and Louise send their love.

      Love,

       Anne

5

Aim

Relating letters of thanks to the learners' own world by using their oral work as input.

Procedure

1 While the pairs are discussing, walk round listening. Write down any useful thanking phrases you hear, or any useful phrases about how the present will be used and any useful vocabulary (see the section on feedback sheets in the Introduction). Write some useful phrases yourself in advance or while the class is doing the exercise.
2 When the pairs have finished discussing, give the phrases to the class for them to write down. Reconstruct the context the phrases were used in.
3 The letter in 5.2 is best written individually in class. Go round monitoring learner output as they write.
4 Upgrade one of the letters (see Introduction) in a later lesson.

6

Aim

Letters of thanks with minimal support.

Teacher input

Letter 1: The learners will need help with this letter. When they have listened to the cassette twice, elicit the basic situation (John and Jim helped Julie to move) and help the learners with the thanking phrase on the cassette ('I don't know what I'd have done without you)'. Let the class imagine exactly how John and Jim helped, but do not insist on too much detail because Julie would not list everything in her letter of thanks. She might, however, mention the meal she cooked for them afterwards. Put the outline of the letter of thanks on the board before the learners start to write. How much you put on the board depends on how good the class is.

Procedure

Letter 2*: This is easier than Letter 1. The learners take notes on the letter in class and write it for homework.

SECTION 3: OFFICIAL WRITING – FORMS, MEMOS AND LETTERS

9 FILLING IN OFFICIAL FORMS

───── **1** ──────────────────────────────

Aim

Understanding official forms and filling them in.

Teacher input

As pre-teaching before Exercise 1, you and the learners list crimes and criminals, for example, 'murder' for crime and 'murderer' for the criminal. The learners write with you as you list the words on the board. This word field will be used again in Unit 20.

Procedure

1 Explain that E.A.P.S. finds jobs for people after they have left prison. Check comprehension of the letters and the Employer's Questionnaire.

2 *Method 1* Learners fill in the form twice, once for each company.

   Method 2 Alternate learners fill in the form for Computerama and Kleenbrite. Then, in pairs, they check each other's forms.

───── **2** ──────────────────────────────

Aim

Filling in personal background information on official forms.

Teacher input

1 If necessary, revise British style addresses and telephone numbers.
2 Learners should work in pairs or small groups. Ask them to look at each photograph and discuss their impressions of the person. Ask what they think of the person in the photograph and list phrases or vocabulary, for example, 'She looks honest', 'He seems nice.'

Procedure

1 Check comprehension of the Client's Questionnaire.
2 For 'Education' (question 4 on the questionnaire) 'secondary school' or 'degree' will do at this stage, although you could do school subjects as a word field if you have time. More detailed CVs are in Unit 11.
3 On the 'Brief personal assessment' section of the questionnaire, single words or phrases are required, not sentences. The Teacher input above should help the learners with the words or phrases.

—— 3 ————————————————————————

Aims

1 Official forms in a commercial/business context.
2 Manipulation of numbers, prices, money.
3 Increased learner input to filling in official forms.

Teacher input

In 3.1 it is important that each learner has a specific (and preferably different) job in a specific company, selling a specific product or working for a specific newspaper. Use real job titles, real companies and products, and newspapers from the learners' own world.

Procedure

Maximum support is given by asking the learners to complete the phrases in 3.2 within the context of the situation, before they start the task.

10 WRITING MEMOS

1

Aims

1 Guided writing for learners to produce their own model memo.
2 Introduction to the company and situation used in Exercises 1, 2 and 3.
3 Showing formal, polite language by contrast.

Teacher input

1 Impoverished English often looks unintentionally rude. Teach the words 'polite' and 'rude'.
2 Poor linking and faulty register make Memo B rude. Explain to the learners that Memo B is rude for the following reasons. First, it uses the imperative without 'please'. It also gives commands without saying why they are necessary, which also sounds rude. Secondly, the description of the new photocopying procedure is in sentences 2 and 4, with the reason for the new procedure between them. It is more polite, with better sentence linking, to put the reason first. Thirdly, 'too many' looks critical and therefore rude.

Procedure

1 Write the four sentences from Memo B on different parts of the board.
2 Ask the learners to rewrite them in the correct order and make them more polite by using 'please' and 'as you know'.

Suggested answer to 1.2

As you know, we have been losing a lot of photocopies and the machine keeps breaking down. For this reason, from now on, if you want to use the photocopier please go to Room 342 and Mrs Clarke will make any copies you need. Please also sign the Photocopying Book and say which department you are from and the purpose of the copies.

—— **2** ——————————————————————

Aims

1 Memo writing with reduced support.
2 Situation B is input to Exercise 3.

Procedure

1 Ask learners as a full class to complete the phrases below Situations A and B. Write as many of the completed phrases on the board as you think the class needs, but do not write everything up for them.
2 Half the class discusses and then writes the memo for Situation A in pairs. The other half discusses and then writes the memo for Situation B.
3 Correct one learner's version of the first memo and one learner's version of the second memo.
4 The learner whose version of the first memo has been corrected dictates it to the half of the class which has not written it. Correspondingly, the learner whose version of the second memo has been corrected dictates it to the half of the class which has not written it.

—— **3** ——————————————————————

Aims

1 Replying to a memo.
2 Writing formal complaints at memo length.
3 Learner input to memos.

Teacher input

1 The learners will need the present perfect tense at this point. The revision of the tense could be combined with useful phrases: 'The photocopier has been on open-access for some time', 'I have always smoked in the office', 'There has been no consultation', 'We have always needed two secretaries in the past.'
2 This is a good upgrading exercise (see Introduction).

Procedure for 3.1

1 Go through the list of grievances with the whole class. Give learners a couple of minutes to make notes on their own about how *they* feel about the problem.
2 Nominate some of the better learners to say how they feel about their grievances. Only do this two or three times. Write useful words and phrases on the board.

3 In the role play learners discuss the grievances in groups. Nominate one person from each group as Group Secretary to make notes on the group's discussion.
4 Each Group Secretary reports his or her group's discussion to you and the whole class. Write further useful words and phrases on the board.

Procedure for 3.2

1 Ask learners to complete the phrases in the context of the situation. Write some of the phrases on the board. Revision of the present perfect could come at this point.
2 The writing of the memo could be done for homework or in class with you checking as they write.

11 WRITING CVs, REPLYING TO JOB AND OTHER ADVERTISEMENTS

1

Aims

1 Revision of letter writing.
2 Answering job advertisements.
3 Describing learners' past in the form of a CV with model.

Procedure

1 1.1 is to be done as a full class. Check comprehension of the advertisement, the CV and the letter.
2 Elicit possible answers to the gapped letter from the learners orally as a whole class. Learners write correct versions as you go along.
3 In 1.2 learners write their own CV and letter in class and you check it as they write. Educational qualifications should be comprehensible to an English-speaking employer but the learners could choose jobs like ski-instructor, lifeguard or au pair where practical experience is more important than qualifications. You could bring in job advertisements from an English language newspaper to give the class ideas, if these advertisements are easily available.

Possible answer to 1.1

Dear Sir, In answer to your *advertisement of/on July 29* I am applying for the post of advertising executive. I have a background in economics. I *read/studied economics* at Bristol University and obtained *a second class honours degree* (please see attached CV). I also have a good *command of* German, as you mention in your advertisement. I am interested in the job because *I want to work abroad / it looks challenging / it looks interesting / it represents a step up from my present job*. I would be happy to attend for interview if selected. Yours *faithfully*, Teresa Price

2

Aims

1 To show the learners some different types of advertisements.
2 Answering advertisements other than job advertisements.

Teacher input

1 Some points of interest from the advertisements:
   i)   In advertisement A 'widower' is one of a limited set of words showing a gender difference in English. Here are some of the most common ones: actress/actor, shepherdess/shepherd, stewardess/steward, waitress/waiter.
   ii) Advertisement B: v.g.c. means 'very good condition', ct means 'caret', M means 'medium', and o.n.o. means 'or nearest offer'. You could ask the learners to speculate why the ring has not been worn.
   iii) Advertisement C: Word field 'Ways of foretelling the future' – horoscopes, tea leaves, crystal balls, Tarot cards.
   iv) Advertisement D: Input to Exercise 4.
   v) Advertisement E: Input to 2.2.
   vi) Advertisements F, G, H: Houses and pets are two aspects of life in Britain. H is input to Exercise 3.
2 Following on from Teacher's Book Unit 5, which discussed letter layout for personal letters, here is some detail on letter layout for official and formal letters.
   i)   The greeting Dear Sir/Madam goes with the ending Yours faithfully. The greeting Dear (+ *first name*) or Dear (+ Mr/Mrs/Miss/Ms + *second name*) goes with the ending Yours sincerely. Dear Ms + *second name* is becoming increasingly common, rather than Dear Mrs + *second name* or Dear Miss + *second name*.
   ii) Dear Sir/Madam and Yours faithfully are used when the addressee is not known by name and are therefore very formal.
   iii) Dear (+ *first and second name*) is an attempt to make a formal situation less formal. For example, if two companies have been dealing with each other for some time, one of them may begin to make the contact less formal in this way.

Answers

2.1 The holiday cottage advertisement is E, the holiday exchange is H, and the lonely hearts are A and D.

2.2 Dear Mr Wilson, In reply to your advertisement / I saw your advertisement in today's newspaper and / I am interested in a holiday at Carpenter's Cottages. Please send me some information / your brochure / further details about the cottages including the cost / the price / for a family of five including two children for a fortnight. Is there a price reduction for children under the age of five? Yours sincerely, Mercedes Sanchez

—— **3** ————

Aim

Relating answering advertisements to the learners' world.

Procedure

Classwork. You help the learners as they write. A good exercise for upgrading (see Introduction).

———— **4*** ————————————————————————————

Aim

Punctuation.

Teacher input

See the notes on punctuation in Teacher's Book Unit 4.

Procedure

Go through the letter in class with the learners. They and you indicate where punctuation is necessary. The learners have the metalanguage for punctuation (comma, full stop, and so on) from the rubric. Feed in as many generalizations from the Teacher input section from Unit 4 as you wish. The letter can then be written for homework.

Answer

Dear Madam,

I read your advertisement in today's Daily Globe with great interest. I'm 22 and a student in my first year at Bristol University studying medicine, so we should have something in common.

I'm interested in music too, though you didn't say what kind of music you like. Personally I like classical music and some jazz. I also go to films whenever I can. I'm afraid I don't like tennis or any other sport much, but I go walking in Leigh Woods a lot. Would that interest you?

I know people think a student's life is full of parties and fun and girls but since I came to Bristol six months ago I have found that it's difficult to really make friends here.

So could we perhaps meet and have a meal together some time? Please give me a ring.

With best wishes,
Yours faithfully,
Richard.

P.S. I've got a car! Do you fancy a drive at the weekend?

——**5** 🔲 ——————————————————

Aim

Free writing with cassette input.

Procedure

Learners listen to all four of the 'lonely hearts'. They listen again and take notes about the person they wish to reply to. The letter can be written as homework or in class. Learners should use the letter in Exercise 4 to help them.

12 LETTERS OF COMPLAINT

1

Aim

Learners construct their own model letter of complaint.

Procedure

In 1.1 help learners to expand the phrases expressing dissatisfaction with products, holidays, train services and so on. The pictures are there only to provide ideas and get the exercise started. Learners should find their own (preferably genuine) examples.

Possible answer to 1.2

Dear Sir,

I wish to complain about my Awayholiday to Amsterdam from 20–27 July this year. We did not 'arrive at the Hook of Holland in time for breakfast' as it says in the brochure. The ferry was on strike and we were not in time for lunch.

We did not stay in the Frans Hals but in a one-star hotel. The breakfast was poor and the service worse.

We did not have time to go to the Rijksmuseum and Anne Frank's house. We also had to pay extra for the visit to the Isle of Marken. The brochure did not say that we had to pay extra.

I think you should refund all the money I paid for this holiday. I look forward to hearing from you.

Yours faithfully,

Tom Lake

2*

Aims

1 Introducing a framework for letters of complaint for use in Exercise 3.
2 Practice in complaining about faulty goods at phrase level.

Procedure

1 Read the section 'To make a complaint' aloud from the leaflet. After each asterisk ask the learners 'Why?'

Example: Teacher: 'Stop using the item.' Why?
Learner: 'Because you must take it back to the shop quickly/ immediately.'

2 Read the section 'If you phone' aloud from the leaflet. After each asterisk ask the learners 'Why?'

3 Read the 'No refunds' box aloud to the learners. Explain 'illegal' and 'faulty'. Ask if a shop can put up a sign saying 'No refunds' in the learners' country(ies). Or is it illegal?

4 Explain 'receipt' and 'guarantee'. A receipt is given by the shop and proves the customer bought a certain item at a certain price on a certain date from that shop. A guarantee is given by the manufacturer and says the manufacturer will repair the item if it is faulty during (usually) the first year.

5 Learners read the chart to themselves and you explain problem vocabulary.

6 Learners fill in the chart alone or in pairs.

Possible answer

Yesterday I bought ...

What?	Receipt or guarantee?	From where?	When I ...	What happened?
b) a TV	both	my electrical goods shop	got it home	I couldn't get a picture
c) a lamb chop	no	my butcher's shop	unwrapped it	it was bad / had gone off
d) a pen	receipt	my stationery shop	tried to write something	it wouldn't write
e) an aeroplane kit	both	my toyshop	got it home	there were no instructions with it
f) a cassette recorder	receipt	my electrical shop	tried to use it	it wouldn't record
g) a toy car	both	my toyshop	gave it to my nephew	one of the wheels fell off

——— 3 ———————————————

Aims

1 Input to situations for Exercise 5.
2 Letter of complaint with reduced support.

Teacher input

1 Learners will need Conditional 2 for the discussion in 3.1. Revise sentences like 'If I hadn't worn it, I would complain' for (a).
2 The situation in (d) recurs in Exercise 4. Teach phrases for this situation. For example, 'disturb me', 'I couldn't get any sleep', 'the noise was deafening', 'a nuisance'.

Procedure

1 In 3.1 discuss each situation with the learners as a full class. Express criteria for complaint as Conditional 2 sentences. For example, 'If he disturbed my work, I would say "Please stop smoking".'
2 Choose one of the situations the learners would complain about and put a model answer on the board, using the framework from 3.2 and eliciting as much of the model as possible from the learners. Make gaps in the model answer by rubbing out some words. Then learners copy the model down, filling in the gaps as they write.
3 Learners choose another situation and follow the instructions for 3.2.

———4 ———————————————

Aims

1 Teaching a 'hope the situation will improve in the future' type of last paragraph.
2 Letters of complaint with minimal support.

Procedure

At least one of the letters can be written as homework provided that learners have taken notes from the cassette in class.

——— 5 ———————————————

Aim

Relating letters of complaint with minimal support to the learners' own world.

Procedure

Input from you and the class at the planning stage of the letter. The letter is then written by learners working alone in class or as homework.

This is a good upgrading exercise (see Introduction).

SECTION 4: EXTENSIVE WRITING – PEOPLE, PLACES AND EVENTS

13 DESCRIBING APPEARANCE

————— 1* —————————————————————

Aims

1 Showing learners different writing styles for describing appearance.
2 Practice of styles possible at this level.

Procedure

1 In 1.1 the task 'Where are the others from?' is given partly to discourage
  a word by word deciphering of the texts. Learners should skim the texts
  and suggest answers as classwork.
2 In 1.2 we see what the learners can do before we start improving it.
  Weaker learners can use style (a) as a model (a list of a pop group's hits,
  for example, would do). Better learners can imitate the letter style of (b)
  or the factual style of (c) or (e). Style (d) may be too difficult for learners
  to use as a model.
3 A good exercise for recycling (see Introduction).

Answers to 1.1

a) Biographical Dictionary (*World Who's Who of Women*)
b) Letter (invented)
c) Autobiography (of George Mikes, humorist)
d) Novel (authentic)
e) Biography (Karl Marx)

————— 2 —————————————————————

Aim

Enriching written description.

Teacher input

Learners should be helped to write an emotional reaction to the people in
the photographs, not just to describe them. Teacher input is, therefore,
vocabulary like: 'trustworthy', 'a kind face' or 'full of life'.

Procedure

1 Stimulus questions like: 'Would she lend a friend £100?' 'Does he like animals?' or 'If he drove into a parked car, would he drive off or report it?'
2 Answers to stimulus questions, combining teacher input with the patterns in the Learner's Book, are written on the board. For example, 'She seems trustworthy', 'I think he's got a kind face'.
3 Learners write three or four sentences about one of the three people in the Learner's Book.
4 A good exercise for recycling or upgrading (see Introduction).

—— **3** ——

Aims

1 Vocabulary for describing faces.
2 Input to describing faces in Exercise 4.
3 Evaluating descriptive phrases (saying which are complimentary).

Answers

a) hook nose
b) curly hair
c) thin lips
d) full lips
e) granny glasses
f) thick glasses
g) wrinkles
h) moustache and beard

—— **4** ——

Aim

Describing faces.

Teacher input

Have some more words or phrases ready for each category (see Possible answers below).

Procedure

Choose one or two learner descriptions of famous people's faces. Discuss them in class with the learners, add to them and upgrade them (see Introduction).

Possible answers

Noses: beaky, like a boxer, snub
Type and colour of hair: redhead, streaked hair, full beard, drooping
  moustache, bushy hair
Complexion: muddy, spotty, clear, beautiful
Evaluation: strong, striking, interesting, attractive, innocent

──── 5 ────────────────────────────────

Aims

1 Describing height and build.
2 Evaluating height and build phrases.

Answers

5.1 a) thin, taller than average
    b) a bit plump
    c) broad-shouldered, stocky, well-built
    d) quite slim
    e) taller than average, broad-shouldered
    f) overweight
5.2 'A little man' and 'overweight' are not complimentary. Change to 'not
    very big' and 'a large man'. Perhaps change 'a bit plump' to 'a nice full
    figure'.

──── 6 ────────────────────────────────

Aims

1 Describing clothes.
2 Order of adjectives.

Teacher input

1 Introduce more words and phrases in each category after learners have
  tried the exercise in pairs (see Possible answers below).
2 The order of the three adjective categories (judgement, colour, material)
  is the correct adjective order.

Possible answers:

Judgement: old-fashioned, neat, expensive, lovely, stunning, pretty
Colour: dark blue, greenish blue, bluey green (these phrases can and
  should, of course, be applied to other colours like 'reddish brown')
Material: linen, woollen (adj.), wool (noun), nylon
Type of clothes: dress, suit, jeans, mac, blouse, skirt, trousers, slacks

——— **7*** ———————————————————————

Aims

1 Consolidation of everything learned in the unit as extensive writing.
2 Another possible upgrading exercise (see Introduction).

Teacher input

1 Revise the simple present tense and adverbs of frequency. For example, 'He usually wears...'
2 Teach 'likes + -ing'. For example, 'She likes wearing...'

14 DESCRIBING PEOPLE, THEIR JOBS AND THEIR LIVES

─── 1 ───

Aim

Extensive writing about people's jobs and lives.

Procedure

1 Ask learners (with their books closed) to write down two occupations each. Write up these headings on the board.
   manual   professional   outdoor   office-based
   involving travel   involving danger
   Elicit occupations from the learners for each category. Write up a few under each heading.
2 In 1.1 learners in groups pick three lists of occupations. Make sure that none of the lists is left out and that learners understand what all the occupations are. They should be clear about the work of a probation officer and a judge.
3 Check that learners have classified the jobs correctly. List the occupations under the headings on the board, finding out each time whether they consider the job is unskilled or skilled.
4 The framework of the model description in 1.3 is:
   Details about the job
   Pay and conditions
   Spare time
      You and the learners discuss one of the occupations using the above framework. Put notes on the board with the degree of support the class needs.
5 Learners read the model description and you explain vocabulary (all the information is genuine, by the way).
6 Learners write about the person they have chosen, either in class or as homework.

─── 2* ───

Aim

Upgrading learners' writing by producing a paragraph related to Exercise 1.

Teacher input

Teach or revise comparison of adjectives. For example, 'a better job' and (for long adjectives) 'a more interesting job'.

Procedure

1 You and the learners choose two jobs and compare them under these (or other) headings:
Salary
Job satisfaction
Variety
Conditions
   The output should be phrases for comparing. For example, *salary:* 'better paid'; *job satisfaction:* 'more interesting'; *conditions:* 'longer holidays'.
2 You and the learners discuss and note reasons for changing jobs. For example, 'he's getting married soon', 'she wants promotion'.
3 You and the learners complete the phrases in the Learner's Book.
4 Learners write the paragraph either in class or as homework.

3

Aim

Describing impressions of people (cassette input).

Procedure

1 Pre-teach the phrases in the Learner's Book.
2 Play the cassette. Learners choose two people to write about.
3 Play the cassette. Learners take notes on the two people they have chosen only. Play the cassette again if necessary.
4 Learners write up the notes as two paragraphs either in class or as homework.

4

Aim

Describing the learners' own world.

Teacher input

Ways of expressing future time. For example, 'I might be ...', 'I will be ...', 'I am going to be ...'.

45

Procedure

1 A limited number of ways of expressing future time are written on the
   board. For example, tentative prediction (may, might, could) and
   definite prediction (will, going to). These are practised in the context of
   the exercise as classwork. For example:
   'I might get a job as a pilot.'
   'I am going to work for a big company.'
   'I will be earning more than I earn now.'
   'I hope I'll be much better at playing the flute.'
   'I may be married and have some children.'
   'I might be living in another country.'
   Learners suggest as many sentences as possible using these patterns.
   There is more work on these ways of expressing future time in Unit 20.
2 Learners do 4.1 and 4.2 as described in the Learner's Book.

15 DESCRIBING PLACES

1

Aims

1 Presenting authentic examples of descriptions of places.
2 Learner input to the authentic examples in the form of evaluating them.
3 Relating describing places to the learners' own world.

Teacher input

1 For 1.1 you might need to tell the learners that Penang is on the west coast of Malaysia or that Estonia is a region of Russia, across the Gulf of Finland from Finland. Tallinn is on the coast.
2 Ask learners in advance to bring in photographs or pictures of their area for 1.3.

Answers to 1.1

1 c	4 d
2 f	5 e
3 b	6 a

Procedure

1 1.2 is a pyramid exercise. Learners in pairs agree a rank order from one to six. They then renegotiate their rank order with another pair, in groups of four. Write up on the board any evaluation phrases this procedure generates.
2 In 1.3 the writing style should be clear and straightforward. We are not aiming to imitate the worst excesses of tourist brochure style. In 1.3 learners should describe only what the place looks like. Detail on local traditions, industries and crafts will follow in the next exercise. 1.3 can, of course, be done as homework.

2

Aim

Writing descriptions of traditions, industries, crafts and politeness customs in the learners' areas at longer than paragraph length.

Teacher input

1 In 2.1 draw up a calendar of events of interest to tourists. For example New Year in January, Carnival in February, and so on. Learners say what happens at each event. If the group is monolingual and from one country you should get a lot of detail from the learners. If many nationalities are represented and the calendar of events varies, get less detail. It would be interesting to include local as well as national traditions.

2 In 2.2 we want general information only. A detailed itinerary follows in Exercise 3, and 2.2 prepares the way by giving the necessary vocabulary.

3 In 2.3 three possible areas of discussion in the Learner's Book are: use of please/thank you, shaking hands, and men/women. (For example, is letting a woman through a door first polite or sexist in the learners' countries?) Other areas are: use of Mr/Mrs/Miss/Ms or first name in conversation, and use of the 'familiar' forms (like 'tu' in French and 'du' in German). Who do you use these forms to? Are they used when praying, and to children as well as to friends? More specific examples, like the 'May I join you?' example in the Learner's Book, should come from the learners.

   Here are some examples, to help the discussion, of what the British view as politeness:
   We say 'sorry' to attract people's attention or just to be polite. It is by no means always a genuine apology. You *could* say 'Is it free?' when you sit down at a table with strangers at a pub. You don't say 'May I join you'. 'You must' and 'You should' are rude in speech but you sometimes find 'you should' in print (learners may have noticed it in Unit 12 Exercise 1). 'Excuse me' can mean 'I want your attention' and it can mean 'I'm sorry' (for example, when you bump into someone).

   The British use first names very freely, so it is not necessarily polite to call someone Mr or Mrs X, just formal. Ms is unusual orally and the combination Mr + first name is wrong. Calling people 'Sir' or 'Madam' is meant to show politeness but it is usually used by shop assistants, hairdressers, car salesmen or other people who deal with customers. If used in everyday conversation it would be too subservient.

   A polite phrase when you give someone something is 'here you are'. You say 'thank you' whenever you receive something (including information). 'Please' accompanies most commands or requests, no matter who you are talking to.

   Lastly, the English language contains relatively few 'formulae', things you always say. Even 'Good morning' is often varied or omitted and 'Good afternoon' and 'Good evening' are becoming rare.

4 In 2.4 remind learners that they are still writing as employees of the Tourist Board.

Procedure

Make as many notes on the board during the discussion in 2.1, 2.2 and 2.3 as the learners need to write the paragraphs in 2.4.

The writing could be homework or classwork.

—— **3** ——————————————————————

Aims

1 Giving information about a town and an itinerary at longer than paragraph length.
2 Revision of letter writing.

Teacher input

1 Explain to the learners that they should *not* find the mistakes first then write the letter in 3.1. This is because we are training the process of selecting the correct language option while writing and not just copying out a corrected text. The time pressure is to build up writing speed.
2 Ask learners in advance to bring in photographs, drawings or pictures of their area for 3.3.

Procedure

1 There should be no pre-teaching in 3.1. Learners rewrite the letter, correcting as they write.
2 The list in 3.2 is, in effect, notes for the writing in 3.3.

Answers to 3.1

(Numbers correspond to the line numbers in the exercise.)
1 *Dear*, not dear
2 *really*, not fairly
3 *to*, not in
4 *lake*, not sea
5 *in*, not of
6 *a cross*, not cross
7 *a donkey*, not donkey
8 *round*, not over
9 *of*, not off
10 *Roman*, not roman
11 *fifteenth*, not fiveteenth
12 *had*, not have
13 *speciality*, not specialism
14 *at*, not by
15 *went*, not go

16 *which*, not what
17 *did some bird watching*, not did bird watching
18 *my*, not our
19 *to*, not for
20 *souvenirs*, not memories
21 *to*, not in
22 *British*, not british
23 *for*, not to
24 *the*, not a
25 *are going to pick*, not will picking
26 *an*, not a
27 *both*, not all
28 *With love* (or *Yours sincerely*) not Yours faithfully

16 NARRATIVE WRITING

───── 1* ───────────────────────────────────

Aims

1 Presenting an authentic example of an anecdote.
2 Input to Exercise 2.

Teacher input

The basic tense for anecdotes is the simple past. The tense and relevant irregular verbs can be revised as necessary.

Possible answers to 1.1

a) I was   f) took it
b) This/It   g) Just as
c) Because   h) road sign
d) I saw   i) deep voice
e) it

Procedure for 1.2

1 Learners as a whole class suggest two or three possible endings to the story. Write key words for each ending on the board, revising the simple past as necessary. For example, Ending 1: 'The police arrested...', 'put him in a...'; Ending 2: 'He explained that...', 'The policeman said...'; Ending 3: 'He drove off...', 'The policeman chased...'
2 You or the learners choose one ending and learners write it, either as classwork or homework; or three groups of learners write one alternative ending each.
3 This is a true anecdote. You may wish to give the learners the true end to the story as a dictation as follows:

───

If you have a road sign in your hand and a policeman asks you where you are going with it, the correct answer is 'I'm taking it to the police station.' 'I thought it would look good in my room,' I said. 'I am arresting you for the theft of this road sign,' the policeman said.

He radioed for a police van, meanwhile holding tight on to my arm. 'Let go,' I said, 'I'm not going anywhere.' The police van, when it came, had seven policemen in it. 'Maybe I look dangerous,' I thought.

At the station they took my fingerprints and checked whether I had a criminal record (I hadn't). They asked if I had any more stolen road signs in my flat. Clearly they thought I was the leader of an international gang of road sign thieves.

They let me phone my mother but held on to my wrist all the time, in case my mother was one of the gang too. Then they put me in a cell while they checked my flat for stolen road signs.

After two hours in the cell I was bored. They wouldn't let me get a book from my car. I asked for a meal. They brought me sausages and chips with a fork and spoon. No knife. Did they think I was going to attack them or kill myself?

Then they let me out. Next day I appeared in court and they fined me £10. I have gone straight since. And Britain's road signs have remained in place.

—— 2

Aim

Writing of anecdotes from the learners' world with minimal support.

Procedure

1 At least some of the anecdote writing should be done in class while you check it. It can be finished for homework.
2 This exercise is strongly recommended for upgrading (see Introduction).

—— 3

Aims

1 Link words.
2 Input to Exercise 4.

Teacher input

The categorization of link words in this exercise is as follows:

The *and* (++) category is when the same thing happened to object 1 and object 2. For example, 'I put the pen and the pencil in the bag' (both things are in the bag).

The *but* (+−) or (−+) category is when something different happened to the second thing. For example, 'I put the pen in the bag but I left the pencil on the table.'

The *so* (→) category is when one thing made another happen, for example, 'I put the bag on the floor, so there's now room on the table.'

Procedure

1 After learners have underlined all the link words in the story (3.1) they fill them in on the chart (3.2). This gives at least one new example for each of the three categories. This helps you to explain the categorization of link words (see Teacher input above).
2 Learners in pairs write new link words in the correct category. You add new link words in the correct category (see Answers below).
3 Unfamiliar link words can be practised and written in the context of the story. For example, 'She worked at night *even though* she had a job during the day.'

Answers to 3.1 and 3.2

(link words in the story)

and (++)	*but* (+−) (−+)	*so* (→)
also	at first ... but then	so
and	but	because
of course	however	

Possible answers to 3.3

(link words not in the story)

and (++)	*but* (+−) (−+)	*so* (→)
in addition (to)	although	therefore
additionally	even though	consequently
too	despite	as a result
moreover	nevertheless	since (not the time reference)
first ... secondly	yet (not the time	
for example	reference)	
then		
still		

——— **4*** ———

Aim

Writing part of an anecdote at paragraph length.

Teacher input

1 Further revision of the simple past tense as necessary, using the story as context.
2 The Possible answer uses a present participle (looking for) to indicate that two actions (eyes on ground and search for necklace) were simultaneous.

53

c

3 Explain 'go back' and 'clear up'.
4 Past perfect (she had lost the necklace) indicates a second, earlier, past event.

Possible answer

She left her tiny room and went back to her friend's house. All the way she kept her eyes on the ground, looking for the necklace. Outside her friend's house she started to cry. There was no sign of the necklace. Through the window she could see into her rich friend's house. She was clearing up after the party. Should she tell her friend that she had lost the necklace? She couldn't. She went home, still crying.

—— **5** ——————————————————————

Aim

Extensive narrative writing, minimal support.

Teacher input

Any vocabulary necessary to the learners' story.

Procedure

1 In small groups, learners think of a story and make notes. You answer learner vocabulary questions.
2 One, two, or three learner stories are elicited, added to and put on the board, still in note form but with as much support as the learners need.
3 Learners write one of the stories from the board or one of their own. They write either in class, with you helping, or as homework.
4 Learner work is upgraded (see Introduction).

17 WRITING ABOUT PUBLIC EVENTS I

1

Aims

1 Help towards eventual decoding of newspaper style in English.
2 Extensive guided writing describing public events.

Teacher input

1 Remind the learners that newspaper style is idiosyncratic in English.
Here are some of the differences between newspaper English and the
sort of standard English the learners are aiming at. (Most of this list is
from R. Quirk *The Use of English*, Longman. See in particular
pp. 174–6.)
a) The use of the indefinite article is idiosyncratic. Quirk gives the
example: 'Mr John William Allaway, a 46-year-old plumber'.
b) People's ages and street addresses are often given.
c) Adjectival clauses are fronted, c.f. 'handsome, bronzed lifeguard Fred
Smith'. This gives sentences an unusual rhythm.
d) There are a large number of journalese words and phrases found
almost exclusively in newspapers. Here are a few: probe, tug of love,
revealed (= made public), condemned (= criticized), mercy dash,
shock.
e) Word order is sometimes idiosyncratic. Quirk quotes this (admittedly
satirical) example: 'Sad-eyed last month was nimble, middle-sized
Life-President Clair Maxwell...'
f) Newspaper headlines use the simple present where we would usually
use the present perfect, c.f. 'Miners go on strike' rather than 'The
miners have gone on strike'.
2 Revise the passive, simple past tense only, c.f. 'Teachers were
offered...', 'McGuire was fined'.

Procedure

Method 1   Classwork. Go through the 'ordinary English' column as
classwork, eliciting answers from the learners. Learners write the paragraph as you go along. This is easier for the learners than Method 2.

Method 2   Groupwork. Half the class works on text A (teachers' pay)

55

and half the class works on text B (tennis). You help while they are working.

Someone from the first group then dictates the teachers' pay text in 'ordinary English' to the half of the class who worked on the tennis text (books closed). Someone from the second group then dictates the tennis text in 'ordinary English' to the half of the class who worked on the teachers' pay text.

Possible answers

Text A   Yesterday Mr Ron Paynter, the leader of the opposition, criticized the 18% pay rise for so-called 'Top People'. He said it was totally unacceptable. The Prime Minister, Mrs Betty Sims, announced the pay rises last week. They are for senior civil servants, judges and other people in leading positions in the country. Teachers were particularly angry about the announcement because they were offered only 7% in recent negotiations. The main teachers' union, the NUT, yesterday threatened to go on strike when negotiations failed. Brian Beak, the teachers' leader, said that the pay rises for Top People are in some cases more than a teacher's entire salary. Ron Paynter agreed with what the teachers were doing. He said he would talk to the pickets who were handing out leaflets at his son's school in Hampstead, London.

Text B   You know John McGuire, the tennis player? He is ranked number one and he's always in trouble. I saw him at Wimbledon last week. He had a row with another player, Juan Lopez. The row was about a service line call. The service machine did not bleep. McGuire said Lopez's service was out. The crowd slow-hand-clapped and booed during the row that followed. In the end McGuire spat at Lopez. I read in the paper that McGuire was fined £20 yesterday. Lopez said the fine was far too small. He said it was a disgrace.

─── 2 ───────────────────────

Aim

Describing and giving a personal reaction to public events (sentence length).

Teacher input

1 Other parts of a newspaper, for example:
   Editorial, crossword, horoscope, Women's Page, weather forecast.
2 Associated newspaper vocabulary, for example: headline, reporter, correspondent.

Answers to 2.1

Sport: b, h, k, p
Home news: c, f, g, m, n, q
Foreign news: a, i, j, o
The arts: d, e, l

Possible answers to 2.2

He won a gold medal. I think he deserves it.
The House of Commons talked about/discussed terrorism again, but when is the government going to do something about it?
The play got an excellent review; I'm delighted.
Have you seen his latest film? It's horrible.
A bomb has exploded in London. It's disgraceful.
There was a bank robbery in Leicester last week. I don't know how they get away with it.
He won in three sets, but I think he was lucky.
The New York subway strike has finished. It's about time.
There's still not enough aid for the famine areas. It's disgraceful.
They were off form. I think they were lucky to win.
She got an Oscar. I don't know how.
There's going to be a government enquiry. It's about time.
Our local trains are running late again. I don't know how they get away with it.
The French franc is up 3%. It's about time.
Arsenal won the match. I think they were lucky.
The terrorists were arrested in London. It serves them right.

--- 3 ---

Aim

Extensive writing: describing and giving a personal reaction to a public event.

Procedure

Take one, two or three of the sentences that the learners wrote in 2.2. As a class, learners add to the story or stories until you have at least enough for them to write a paragraph. You put notes on the board on the one, two or three stories at the level of support the class needs.

The learners write one, two or three stories with a personal reaction. The whole class could write one story or learners could choose which story they want to write.

The writing can be done in class or as homework. A good exercise for upgrading (see Introduction).

───── **4** ──────────────────────────────────

Aim

Increased learner input to writing about public events.

Teacher input

As illustrated earlier, newspaper style is particularly idiosyncratic in English, and learners are not being asked to imitate it. They should imagine that they saw the newspaper article complete and are writing about it to an English-speaking friend.

Note Any answer is possible, the more imaginative the better, so no model answer is given.

18 WRITING ABOUT PUBLIC EVENTS II

——— **1*** ———————————————————————

Aims

1 Vocabulary input for describing and reacting to public events.
2 Building up writing speed at paragraph length and above.
3 Drawing learners' attention to linking.
4 Guided writing above the learners' estimated free writing level.
5 Drawing learners' attention to author attitude in texts.

Teacher input

Explain to the learners that this exercise develops speed and fluency in writing, so they are asked to write a text out rather than marking the correct choices.

Procedure

1 A third of the class write about crossing the Atlantic in a powerboat, a third about long distance flying in a hot air balloon, and a third about climbing the most Alpine mountains in a week.
2 One learner from each of the three groups reads the story aloud to the whole class. This is to develop the learners' feeling for sentence rhythm in English.

Answers

In the answers below links are underlined and places where the author shows an attitude are boxed.

This week there was an attempt to break the world record for crossing the Atlantic in a powerboat. The crew of the 'Blue Wave' are all experienced sailors. Their attempt is being sponsored by AFB, who make nautical equipment and boats among other things. I suppose they want the publicity, and nobody asked the crew to risk their lives. But something about these 'stunt' world record attempts still worries me. I mean, the total cost of all this 'fun and games' on the water is over £250,000. You could build a hospital or a school for that. And there have been │ dozens │ of record attempts like <u>this</u>. The │ public is bored │ with <u>them</u>. (The attitude is negative and critical.)

This week there was an attempt to break the world record for long distance flying in a <u>hot air balloon</u>. Three students from Cambridge are taking their pet dog with them <u>into the clouds</u>. One of the <u>trio</u> apparently said that the animal doesn't mind <u>heights</u> as long as it doesn't rain. │ I thought <u>that</u> was rather funny, │ but I hope he <u>still likes</u> <u>heights</u> when he comes down from the <u>clouds</u>! Apparently they are taking champagne and strawberries and cream <u>up there</u> with them. │ <u>It</u> all looked so ridiculous on telly last night! │ <u>They</u> were even making the <u>dog</u> wave its <u>paw</u> as they │ disappeared out of sight. │ (The attitude is lighthearted and amused.)

This week there was an attempt to break the world record for climbing the most <u>Alpine mountains</u> in a week. Chris Hetherington, who has led several <u>expeditions</u> in the <u>Himalayas</u>, is someone │ I admire a great │ deal. │ │ I think he's got a lot of courage, │ but I hope he hasn't bitten off more than he can chew this time <u>because</u> he's pushing fifty now. <u>Still</u>, │ it would be marvellous │ if he could do it. │ A real contribution │ to Britain's achievement in this field. (The attitude is respectful and patri- otic, some would call it sycophantic.)

──── **2** ────────────────────────────────

Aim

Relating descriptions of public events to the learners' world.

Note The sexist assumption that the visitor is male was to avoid too many him/her and he/she's in the limited space of the boxes, and to avoid using words like spouse. By all means make the visitor a woman if you like.

Procedure

Homework. A good exercise for upgrading. This exercise gives learners the chance to individualize their writing, so no model answer is given here.

—— **3** ————————————————————————

Aims

1 Register switching from newspaper English to the sort of English written in a letter to a friend.
2 Input for 3.3.

Procedure

1 Underline errors in learners' writing in 3.1 before the learners attempt 3.3. Do not correct the errors.
2 Learners are made familiar with a slightly different version of the train crash in 3.2.
3 In 3.3 they write about the new version of the train crash. Their paragraph from 3.1 with your underlining is returned to them before they start writing. In their new version of the train crash they have to avoid the errors you underlined in their 3.1 version.

Possible answers to 3.1

1 thought to be / I think
2 happened
3 At first everybody thought
4 even more people would have been hurt
5 who lives in
6 praised / the police said she did well
7 *omit age*, who lives in

Possible answers to 3.2

(Newspaper report first in each case.)
1 killing two people and injuring three / several local people were hurt
2 the 11 o'clock train / the 9 o'clock train
3 Frances Bradshaw / Barbara Bradshaw
4 Mrs Bradshaw ... trained in First Aid / interested ... programme on TV about First Aid
5 third train crash / second accident
6 in six months / in the last year
7 Bradshaw ... signed the petition / if I saw one I think I'd sign

Note If the driver had had a heart attack (newspaper report) he *might* not have been able to slow down (radio interview).

⤜⤜➤

Answer to 3.3

Note   The learners' answers should contain this information.

There was a train crash near Oxford when the 9 o'clock passenger train hit a stationary goods train. Two local people were heroes. Stephen Buckley pulled injured people out of their compartments and Barbara Bradshaw gave them First Aid. The police later praised Mrs Bradshaw for her treatment of the injured.

There is a petition protesting against the dangers of the line at that point. Stephen Buckley has signed it and Mrs Bradshaw said she would sign it.

SECTION 5: EXTENSIVE WRITING – EVALUATION AND OPINION

19 EVALUATION IN WRITING

Note Learners should prepare Exercises 1 and 4 in advance.

——— **1** ————————————————————————

Aims

1 Relating books, films, TV and plays to the learners' world and establishing basic vocabulary.
2 Revision of question forms.

Teacher input

1 Ask the learners to write at least some of the quiz questions in advance of the lesson, so they can use reference books.
2 Question words are 'does' (simple present, third person), 'do' (simple present) and 'did' (simple past). Question words are not used:
   a) when 'who', 'what' or 'which' is the subject (not the object) of the sentence;
   b) when there is an auxiliary verb like 'have', 'be' or any modal ('can', 'may', 'might', etc.).

Procedure

1 If the learners have not written the quiz questions in advance (as requested!) they write them in pairs in class.
2 A few learners read out questions and you write them on the board to revise the formation of questions in English. The board looks like this:

With a question word	Without a question word
simple present: Does (*learner's question*)? (third person)	Who (*learner's question*)? who/what/which as subject
simple present: Do (*learner's question*)?	Has (*learner's question*)? have/be
simple past: Did (*learner's question*)?	Can (*learner's question*)? modals

You may have to supply questions to illustrate the 'have/be' and 'modals' pattern. For example: 'Has there been a film of the German novel *The Tin Drum?*' Answer: 'Yes, it was directed by Volker Schlörndorf.' 'Can a producer also direct a film?' Answer: 'Yes, Woody Allen has co-produced and directed as well as starred in several of his films.'

3 Learners or learners in pairs give their questions to others in the class to answer.
4 You write further examples of questions and vocabulary. (See the section on feedback sheets in the Introduction.)

------- 2 -------

Aim

Information transfer (of evaluation phrases in formal register).

Procedure

After learners have done the exercise ask them which phrases can be applied to books, which to films and TV, which to plays and which to all of them.

Suggested answer

Note Allow any reasonable answer.

Praise	*Criticism*
an excellent production	hopeless
totally convincing	terrible
very moving	banal
hilariously funny	obvious
the acting was superb	the characterization was poor
magnificently shot	the plot was incredibly bad
the character development was good	full of clichés
X played the part of Y well	the story was unbelievable
the set was beautiful	the characters were inconsistent
quite moving	the plot developed slowly
believable	

------- 3 -------

Aims

1 Relating evaluation of films, plays or books to the learners' world.
2 Structuring extensive writing.

Teacher input

Learners are expected to write three or four paragraphs. There are no 'rules' for paragraphing a text, but poor paragraph layout looks bad, so learners should start a new paragraph every six or seven lines.

Procedure

1 Rather than imposing a structure on learners' writing in advance, collect in the learners' notes before they start writing the paragraphs and change the order if necessary. (Tell learners you are going to do this and ask them to write clearly.)
2 The writing can then be done in class and you can work on organization and structure with weaker learners while the better ones start the writing. Even with a large class, writing is a sufficiently slow activity for you to monitor everyone at least once during the course of a lesson. Check what they have written and ask them what they intend to write next. Keep a note of any errors they make. (Use a feedback sheet as described in the Introduction.)
3 Next lesson, if necessary, you can analyse the structure of some of the better pieces of writing and they can become the model for the next long piece of writing.

—— **4** ———————————————————————

Aim

Description and evaluation of a TV programme at longer than paragraph length.

Procedure

For groups which cannot watch TV programmes in English: A series (particularly a soap opera) that most of the learners watch regularly is ideal. You might like to do one of the presentations or an extra presentation yourself.
For groups which can watch TV programmes in English: The learners are going to require more support from you. You will have to watch the programme yourself. The learners must choose a programme that is 30 minutes long (or shorter). Ideally, get the learners to watch the programme with an English-speaking person who can help them understand it. Soap operas are best, preferably a soap that you know and like yourself.

——**5** 📼 ————————————————————————

Aim

A short paragraph evaluating music.

Procedure

1 Elicit more evaluation phrases for music by asking learners which of the evaluation phrases in the unit so far could be applied to music.
2 Play each piece of music on the cassette and give the learners time to write their reactions to it (three or four sentences).
3 Learners read out what they have written and you correct it orally; they make the corrections in writing.
4 You and the learners list different kinds of music and learners use the evaluation phrases they have learned to say why they like or dislike them.

20 OPINION IN WRITING

———— 1 ————————————————————

Aims

1 Showing learners the language of expressing opinion contrasted with other functions.
2 Input to Exercises 2, 3 and 4.

Answers

Opinions: a) c) f) h) i) j) k) l)
b) statement of fact   d) definition   e) example   g) interpretation of facts

———— 2 ————————————————————

Aim

Extensive writing about the future.

Teacher input

1 Two of the ways of expressing future time are:
   a) Tentative prediction (you are not sure) with modals, may, might, could, e.g. 'Russia may/might/could find more oil'.
   b) Definite prediction (you are sure of your opinion) with 'will' or 'going to', e.g. 'The 1990s will / are going to be difficult', 'If we cooperate, things will get better'.

Note   These are the two classifications suggested for this exercise. The same classification was used in Unit 14.
2 The second quotation is ambiguous. James Baldwin (the black American novelist and author of *Go Tell It On the Mountain*) may have meant that the future belongs to black people, or the quotation may mean 'black' in the sense of 'negative'. Choose either option, or both.

Procedure

1 At least one person from each group makes notes on the group's

discussion of the quotations. You listen to the discussion and use a feedback sheet (see Introduction).

2 Elicit predictions from the learners as a whole class. Write predictions on the board using the classification suggested above and exemplifying every case (may, might, could, will, going to) with as many learner examples as possible. Feed in vocabulary and anything else from the feedback sheet.

3 If necessary, help the learners plan the two to four paragraphs of their writing.

4 The writing may be done as homework.

—— **3** ————————————————

Aim

Extensive writing about sentencing for crime.

Teacher input

1 Modals 'should' or 'ought to' + infinitive without 'to' to express opinion, e.g. 'There should be a heavy sentence for robbery.'

2 The word field crime and criminals came up in Unit 1. Work done then could be revised.

Procedure

1 Use a feedback sheet (see Introduction) during the group discussion phase in 3.2.

2 Discuss the feedback sheet with the group and (if necessary) help plan the three or four paragraphs of writing before 3.3.

3 The writing may be done for homework.

Answers

In Britain: *soliciting:* £10 first conviction, £25 second conviction, £25 and 3 months prison for third and subsequent convictions; *bigamy:* 7 years; *suicide:* not a crime; *forgery:* at the discretion of the court; *theft:* not more than 10 years; *destroying or damaging property:* not more than 10 years; *handling stolen goods:* not more than 14 years; *murder:* imprisonment for life; *blackmail:* not more than 14 years; *performing an obscene play:* £400 fine or 6 months; *burglary with a firearm:* life imprisonment; *possession of drugs:* it depends on the drug; *rape:* not more than 7 years.

——**4** ————————————————————

Aim

Writing about other people's opinions and your own at above paragraph
length (cassette input).

Procedure

1 While listening to the cassette the learners could have some or all of the
following phrases from the cassette on the board, if you think they need
the support. The phrases are in order of utterance on the cassette: a
radio phone-in programme, Home Secretary, crime wave, steps, we
intend to be firm, maximum sentence, assault, Customs Officers, drug
dealers, more force, the underlying causes of crime, unemployment,
poverty, tackle the real reasons, in percentage terms, mounting a
campaign, security locks, bring back the death penalty, hanging,
morally wrong, personal judgement.

2 The opinions on the cassette are summarized below. Learners should
add their own views in each section.

Reasons for the increase in crime and how to stop it
be firm; increase maximum sentences for assault and rape (Carlisle)
underlying causes unemployment and poverty (Pinner)
unemployment *not* a cause of crime (Carlisle)
'Lock It' campaign (Carlisle)

Why people turn to drugs and how to stop them
increase Customs Officers; try to catch drug dealers (Carlisle)
more police, increase police pay (Pinner)
kids feel they have no future so take drugs (Pinner)
TV campaign on drugs (Carlisle)

The death penalty for serious crimes
number of murders increased since death penalty abolished (Jordan)
number of murders has not increased since death penalty abolished
  (Carlisle)
not a deterrent (Carlisle)
wrong men have been hanged (Carlisle)
morally wrong (Carlisle)

—— **5** ————————————————————————

Aim

Writing about marriage at longer than paragraph length.

Teacher input

It is important to point out to the learners that they are asked to guess what the stories could be about purely to generate ideas about the subject of marriage. (D in particular is almost impossible to guess and the learners should not feel cheated when they fail to guess it.)

Procedure

When the learners have guessed what the stories could be about you should tell them the real stories, with as much or as little detail as you wish. It would be best to make brief notes on the board about the stories.

――― **A** ―――――――――――――――――――――――――――

Bride dies hours after hospital wedding (*The Times*, 28 May 1985)

A woman of 22 knew that she was dying of cancer. She knew that she had only hours to live. She had known her boyfriend since she was fourteen and the two of them decided to marry.

They married in hospital and nurses pushed two beds together so the couple could spend their wedding night in each other's arms. The woman wore a wedding dress borrowed from a nurse as there wasn't time to have one made.

During the night they discussed the arrangements for the funeral. She died the next day.

――― **B** ―――――――――――――――――――――――――――

American women are branching out into big business. Missionaries of womanpower spread the success gospel. (*The Times*, 3 June 1985)

American women have formed a trade mission called US Women in Exporting. The women run companies in areas like high technology, telecommunications, tourism, insurance, health care, business services, training and recruiting.

In Britain, too, the number of self-employed women has risen by 24% to half a million. The American women gave the following advice to women elsewhere who want to start up on their own.

Janel Landon, 35, president of a Chicago travel management company: 'The biggest problem women have is balancing home and office. We have to learn ... that it's OK to spend only four or five hours with the kids. In America more and more women are hiring home managers. They buy the groceries, plan the meals, coordinate the children's after-school activities and see that the home runs smoothly.' Janel's husband, Wayne, joined her company two years after she set it up.

Thomasine Tarsell, 43, president of Tomco Insurance Corporation and Tomco Money Management Corporation: 'People entrust their lives, businesses, families and estates to insurance companies and when they put that kind of confidence in you, you should take it seriously. The price? Well, my own ambition cost me my second marriage. I'm not married now. I'm not a mother. I have opportunities to do the things I want to do.'

C

Declarations of independence. More and more people are choosing to live alone. What is the singular attraction? (The Times, 17 April 1985)

If the trend of the past two decades continues, 80% of households will be either single people or family groups headed by a single person by the end of the century. In Australia 4% of the adult population was unmarried in the 1960s. In the 1980s it was 25%.

Being single is no longer associated with failure to find a marriage partner. It is now more often associated with strength and individuality.

Asked about the advantages of being single many women said not having to cook an evening meal and not having to watch sport on TV. Many married people also keep single lifestyles. For example, when the novelist Margaret Drabble married biographer Michael Holroyd they kept their separate houses and still spend time alone in them.

It is more socially acceptable for the job or career to replace marriage, especially for women. Single people said the following:

Susan Egerton-Jones, 45, senior publisher, has never felt a maternal urge. Holidays with men usually kill any marriage plans because she wants to go and see cathedrals and they want to stay in bed. Most evenings she has a snack alone in front of the telly with her cat.

Mark Todd, 30, won a gold medal for New Zealand at eventing (horse-riding) at the Los Angeles Olympics. His white Mercedes has an 'I love my horse' sticker in the back window. He says he travels too much to marry and anyway, 'I've always been a little scared of marriage. My parents have such an ideal one, I'm worried I might not be able to achieve the same.' When he did think of marriage it was the women who broke it off. Perhaps women are making most of the running at the singles game.

D

Politicians and happy marriages (The Times, 15 April 1985)

Three politicians, Margaret Thatcher, Neil Kinnock and David Steel gave advice on how to have a happy marriage. The advice was in a British Medical Association free booklet called 'Getting Married'.

Mrs Thatcher said, 'The warmth of your family and keeping that relationship bright and alive will mean more to you than anything else.'

Glenys and Neil Kinnock said, 'Being friends is the most important thing. It means that you can be frank with each other so that small disagreements don't build up into big rows.'

Judy and David Steel said, 'Make sure that all your decisions are joint ones.'

TAPESCRIPT

2

Tim: Joanna don't go on at me, please. I'm trying. I wrote off for three jobs this morning.

Joanna: That's not what I mean, and you know it. It's you I'm worried about. Not jobs, not money. You. I think we should go back to the Timeplan.

Tim: Oh lord.

Joanna: Tim! You're getting fat. You're drinking too much. And you aren't spending any time with the kids.

Tim: I haven't got time.

Joanna: Timeplan. Here it is. We start again.

Tim: OK.

Joanna: Right, swimming.

Tim: I'm not going to Leytonstone, it's too far.

Joanna: OK. One of the others. Sunday morning?

Tim: OK.

Joanna: And what about taking Tracy swimming?

Tim: She doesn't want to go with me.

Joanna: Going swimming with you was the high point of her week! Until you stopped going. Waterfun. When? Saturday?

Tim: Yes.

Joanna: OK. I'm writing this down, Tim. Saturday and Sunday. Same pool.

Tim: Roger phoned about playing squash. It'll have to be lunchtime, as he's got a job. Say 12 o'clock.

Joanna: Um, Friday?

Tim: No. Er, make it midweek. Wednesday.

Joanna: And what about the gym? You used to go every day.

Tim: Is this really necessary? OK, OK. Put the gym down for Monday and Friday. I'll do an hour before it closes. When there's nobody there.

Joanna: Gym. Monday and Friday. Right.

Tim: And I'll challenge you to a game of tennis.

Joanna: Me? I haven't played for years.

Tim: Come on. I'm not the only one getting fat.

Joanna: Oy! Very well then. Um, every Tuesday? When Tracy gets home from school. Say five till six? Where? Ridgeway?

Tim: No. I don't want to walk up the hill.

Joanna: There speaks the great sportsman. OK, War Memorial then. What about Thursday, what are you going to do on Thursday?

Tim: I'm going to spend Thursday in the bath.

Joanna: That's my Tim!

Tapescript

Unit 3 ————————————————————————————

5

Postcard One *From Ian to Sandy*

Ian: It's so busy here, Sandy. Everything's so exciting.

Guide: Welcome to the Lincoln Centre. This tour lasts approximately forty-five minutes. On your left you can see early paintings by the Russian born painter Marc Chagall...

Ian: Really good, trad jazz. That's what I like. I've never heard it played so well. Eh? What? Oh, a bourbon on the rocks, please.

Man: Oh, you're from Scotland. I was in Scotland in '85. Had a great time. Hey, why don't ya come over and have a meal tonight? Wife'll be thrilled to meet you.

Postcard Two *From Jean to her sister Jackie*

Jean: Suntan oil. Where's the suntan oil? I put it in the basket, I'm sure I did.

Marco: Excuse me. Have you lost something?

Jean: What? Oh. I can't find my suntan oil.

Marco: Oh dear. I think I have some. Just one moment please.

Jean: No. It's ... Oh, all right.

Marco: You are the most beautiful girl in the world. You are my sun and moon and your eyes are my stars.

Jean: Oooh heck! Oh, I'm so happy! Oh, Marco!

Postcard Three *From Arthur and Doris to Fred*

Instructor: Don't forget. Lean forward. Don't forget. Bend the knees.

Doris: Arthur. I don't like it. Look, he's fallen over. I said we should have gone to Clacton.

Instructor: Next please. Doris. Come on, bend the knees.

Doris: Ooooh!

Doris: Oooh Arthur, isn't it lovely? Look at the sun glinting on the snow.

Instructor: Thank you, thank you, thank you ... And a special prize in the beginners' section. Wait please. It wasn't the fastest downhill run ... And she fell over once or twice ... The special prize is for the most courageous downhill run. It goes to a grandmother, sixty-five-year-old Mrs Doris Davies from London.

Doris: Oooh Arthur! Oh, that's me!

Unit 4 ————————————————————————————

5

Man: It was not like a prison at all. We were in small huts, only three people to a hut and there were video cameras and microphones everywhere. They put things in the food to make us sleep a lot. When we left the hut a guard followed us. The guards were everywhere, there were hundreds of them. The only time we saw the others was exercise time once a day. If we were careful, we could write notes to them. Number seven had the idea for the escape. He passed me a note about clothes. During the next week, or maybe month, number nine passed me a note about passports and number twenty-one passed me a note about guns. Guns. Guns.

Yes. I read the notes in a corner of the hut where the video cameras couldn't see me. We escaped six months later, or maybe it was a year. We were dressed in suits. Seven paid some women to bring the cloth in and he and his team made the suits with wooden needles. They made them in their beds at night. Nine and his group made passports from writing paper and cardboard boxes. The guards gave us the ink. We said we wanted it for the art class. The art class.

When we escaped we put a gun into a guard's back and made him cut the wire. The gun was made of wood. Wood. Twenty-one and his group used one of the bread knives to make it. So we got outside. We escaped. But outside there was no town. There was no city. There was no jungle. Just a tape recorder with jungle noises and more guards, laughing...

Unit 7

3

Alan:	Hello. My name's Alan Wicks. The writer of this English book, Michael Dean, asked me to tell you about Chantal. I'd just come down from Cambridge University, in my first year, for a reunion with people from my old school. Frank Simpson and I arranged to go for a drink afterwards. I've known Frank all my life, by the way. He told me about Chantal then. She'd come to Northampton as an au pair. Anyway, the first time I met her was at a disco. We got chatting...
Alan:	My name's Alan. I'm at Cambridge University.
Chantal:	Chantal. Oh, you must be very clever!
Alan:	Oh ... well. Actually, a few of us are going on to a club after this finishes. Sort of a group. Why don't you come along?
Chantal:	I don't know. I've got to be back by eleven o'clock. I haven't got a key.
Alan:	I thought I'd better say it was a group or she wouldn't come. Then I had to find a group of people. Mike Dean was one of them. He was in Northampton for the summer. Anyway, that night at the club I asked Chantal out for a meal at a steak bar the following Saturday. I borrowed the money from my dad. Then we took a bus out to some of the villages near here. And I took her for a day trip round my college at Cambridge. I wanted to see her every day, but she said no. The time was so short. She was only in Northampton for her school holidays. She was still at school, you see. I didn't know Frank was interested in her at all.
Frank:	Oh come on, Al. This is Frank Simpson. Actually, I took Chantal out before Alan did, though I didn't tell him that. We went to Brights, a nightclub in Northampton. I picked her up in the Rover and we danced till two o'clock in the morning. The family she was staying with weren't all that pleased! Then what did we do? We cooked food together for a

picnic. She watched me play football every week. We went for some long drives. As far as Coventry once to see the cathedral. We had fun. That's all. Nobody took it seriously.

Chantal: So what was I supposed to do? It was so exciting with Frank but I wasn't sure if I loved him. One day we walked along the river in Northampton and talked and I thought I was sure. But the next day ... And Alan cared for me so much and he's so sensitive. I didn't want to hurt him.

Alan: Hello, darling. This is Alan.

Chantal: Oh hi, Alan. I was just washing my hair.

Alan: I was wondering ... Look, could I possibly see you tonight? We could go for a walk. Or I'll try and borrow dad's car. Look, I tell you what, let's go to the cinema.

Chantal: The cinema? Oh Alan, I'm afraid I'm going out this evening.

Alan: What? Who with? *I* asked you. I asked you last week. Chantal what are you trying to do to me?

Chantal: He rang off in the end. I tried to phone him back but his father wouldn't let him speak to me. He said Alan had been crying. So I wrote. I asked Alan to my party. Of course, I asked Frank too. But Alan thought he was *with* me at the party. When I danced with Frank he went mad. I thought they were going to fight. The party was a nightmare. The next day, after my English lesson, I asked my teacher, Mike, if he thought I had done anything wrong. He said he thought it wasn't my fault. I felt a bit better after that.

Unit 7

4

Chantal: By the autumn of that year I felt sure I loved Frank. I kept remembering the way he held me close at that last party in July. We wrote to each other. In his letter he said the party had been wonderful for him too. I invited him to Paris for Christmas. I kept imagining him meeting my parents. I lived it all in my mind. Showing him Paris. Going on a boat trip on the Seine (yes, even in December). Going to the special little restaurants and bars, the art galleries, well, you know.

Frank: Look. Let's have one thing clear. It was a holiday romance and I never said it was anything else. Never, not once. Chantal wrote every week, seemed like every week anyway. I think I wrote back once. Thanked her for the party. In November I met a local girl and we got engaged. We're going to Paris for our honeymoon funnily enough. Another funny thing is she's tall with long black hair, just like Chantal.

Chantal: Of course, I was hurt, at first. Of course, I cried. And then I thought, well, that's life. Alan was still writing to me so I thought, why not. And I asked him to come to Paris instead of Frank. And do you know what happened, over Christmas ...

Unit 8

6

Conversation One

Julie: I think that's everything, I hope. Oh, I don't know what I'd have done without you.

John: Julie, Jim says do you want the big table in this room or upstairs?

Julie: Oh.God!

John: It's OK. Jim and me'll do it. But where do you want it?

Julie: Upstairs. Cheers, John, you're wonderful.

John: True, true. I'll help you put the curtains up in a minute. Or should we clean the floor first?

Julie: Um, no, forget the floor. We'll do the curtains and then we'll move the cooker. At least I can make you all a meal.

Jim: Julie, where's the fridge? It's not still in the old house, is it?

Julie: Oh God!

Conversation Two

Klaus: Is this a book? Yes, it is. Is this a book? No, it isn't. Is this a book or a pen? It's a pen. Surely. Yes, it's definitely a pen. It looks like a biro. So why are they asking? Alexander, can you come here a minute?

Alexander: Yes, Klaus. What's the problem?

Klaus: It's my son's English homework from school. Can you give me a hand with it please?

Alexander: Sure.

Klaus: Thanks. This is all Greek to me.

Unit 11

5

Host: Hello. Welcome to 'Friendship and Possibly Love', the radio programme where people who want to meet other people get the chance to do so. And if you'd like to meet one of our guests this evening, just pick up a pen and write to the person of your choice. And our first guest this evening is Michelle. Michelle is twenty-three and she's from Cardiff. She's about five foot four and weighs seven stone six. So much for the statistics. Tell us about yourself, Michelle.

Michelle: My name is Michelle Morgan, as he said and I'm from Cardiff in Wales. Well, I got divorced last year, you see. And so I thought I'd come here, er, come on this programme. It's difficult with my job actually, seeing, er, meeting anybody new. That's the problem. Or you meet the wrong type, you know.

Host: You have a son, haven't you?

Michelle: That's right. Lloyd, he's five.

Host: And how long were you married?

Michelle: Er, I got married when I was sixteen, you see. That's all I knew, Jack

	and the house and then Lloyd. Jack drives a minicab, he lives ... well, I still see him. But that was all I knew. I mean I haven't even been to a dance since I was fifteen.
Host:	Do you work now Michelle?
Michelle:	Oh yes! I got myself a job. Well, it's only a little job down Frank's ... down at the cafe. Waitress. But my mother-in-law's a big help. Ex-mother-in-law. She comes in and takes care of Lloyd, you know. It's funny. I feel like I just been born. I don't know anything. I don't know any people much. Jack wasn't ... you know, didn't mix. But I want to come out in the world now. I want to meet people. I want to live. You know. Start my life I suppose.
Host:	... and write if you want to meet Michelle. And our next guest is Wendy Palmer-Green from Beckenham, Kent. Wendy is thirty and runs her own Dog Clipping and Grooming business. She's five foot eight, doesn't want me to say how much she weighs but doesn't mind if I say she's a very attractive lady. Is that right, Wendy?
Wendy:	Yes, that's more or less correct, yes.
Host:	Well, now, tell us a little bit, first of all, about your – your Dog Clipping and Grooming business. How long have you been running that?
Wendy:	Um, I've been running it for about eight years. I set up my own business, um, and in that business I'm afraid I don't come into contact with many men. It's mostly little old ladies who bring in their poodles to be clipped and groomed. And, unfortunately, um, I just don't meet men.
Host:	But you must have quite a lot of spare time.
Wendy:	I have got spare time, yes, in the evenings. My hobbies are music and art. Um, and those are fairly lonely pursuits as well, so I just don't come into contact with men at all ...
Host:	... so why not write if you want to meet Wendy. And sitting next to me now is Grant Gregson. Grant is twenty-five and he was born in London. He's six foot one, weighs thirteen stone seven and he's a fit, well-built man. Grant. Tell us about yourself.
Grant:	Thanks, Terry. My name's Grant Gregson. You may have heard the name. I'm a professional tennis player, ranked number nine in Britain at the moment. You may have seen me on telly. My first round match with McEnroe was on BBC2 last Wimbledon.
Host:	Who won?
Grant:	Well, he did. He usually does, you know.
Host:	Three straight sets, wasn't it? Six one, six one, six love.
Grant:	Look, I didn't come here to talk about tennis. OK? I'm here to talk about myself.
Host:	Excuse me. Go on.
Grant:	Right. So, I, er, meet plenty of girls on my travels round the world. And I've had a lot of girlfriends, including some of the top women tennis players, who you'll have heard of. No names mind! So I'm looking for a girl now who doesn't play sport, especially tennis, and who maybe isn't even interested in tennis.
Host:	Do you think you'll get married one day? If you found the right girl?
Grant:	Right. That's been the problem. It's all been one night stands, you know. Kiss and goodbye. I want to ...
Host:	... ring us here on 'Friendship and Possibly Love' as usual if you want to

78

meet Grant. Our next guest is Sid Shandy. Sid is eighteen and he's from Birmingham. Sid's five foot nine and weighs about eleven stone. All yours, Sid.

Sid: All right, Tel. Um, well, basically I just wanted to say that I've moved to a different area now – I used to live in Birmingham, now I live in Wolverhampton – and I wanted to try and meet some new people in the Wolverhampton area because you know, as I say, I've just moved here and I'm a bit, a bit lonely.

Host: What do you do?

Sid: Well, I don't do anything at the moment. I was an apprentice in, for British Leyland, which is the car factory, but I got made redundant, you know, sort of last in, first out. So, I haven't got a job at the moment but I'm very hopeful if I get something now I've moved to Wolverhampton.

Host: Good. Do you have any hobbies, Sid?

Sid: I like football. Support Birmingham City. Um, I like to play football in the Sunday league and I like going to the pub with me friends...

Unit 12

4

Conversation One

Man 1: Last week all these noises came from the flat above during the night. I can't stand any more. I'm going to write to the couple in the flat and complain. Their names are John and Margaret Jameson. Here are the noises. Monday (*dog barking*). Tuesday...

Man 2: Where is it?

Woman: I don't know!

Man 2: Well, where can it be?

Woman: I said I don't know! Are you deaf?

Man 2: You *must* know.

Woman: Well, I don't.

Man 2: Oh, I've had enough!

Man 1: And then on Wednesday (*baby crying*). And on Thursday (*loud music*). And on Friday...

Woman: You don't love me! You don't love me! You don't love me!

Man 2: That's right! I don't.

Man 1: They don't answer the door when I ring. I've had no sleep for a week. My wife is tired, I'm tired. So I'm going to write and complain.

Conversation Two

Don: Hello, Jean. Jean, what's wrong?

Jean: It's Martin. Have you seen him?

Don: No, what's happened?

Jean: He's just come in from school. He's got blood on his face. He was in the bathroom trying to wash it off. He didn't want me to see it.

Don: Blood. Oh. So the other kids hit him again.

Jean: Yes, Don. Again. The third time this week.

Don: He's got to learn to fight for himself, Jean.

Jean: Don, he's six years old. And there were three boys who hit him. All of them bigger than Martin.

Don: What do you want me to do?

Jean: I've got the boys' names. Martin didn't want to tell me. But I made him. And I've found their addresses in the telephone directory.

Don: You want me to speak to their parents?

Jean: Perhaps. But they live miles away. Let's write to them first.

Don: Do you think that will help?

Jean: Don, let's write to them before their kids kill our Martin.

Unit 14

3

Man 1: Cynthia? Oh, her, yes. She looks awful, doesn't she? No, I mean, no, I'm not being rotten, it's just that she works far too hard. Just too, um, conscientious. Mind you, they pay her, I mean she's paid well enough. But money isn't everything. You'd think she could afford something better than that dress. Yellow with green spots – look great in the jungle but here ... I suppose she thinks because she's tall and fairly pretty she can get away with anything.

Woman 1: Oh God, he's gorgeous!, Oh I'm going all weak at the knees ... What do you mean a midget! Don't be bloody rude, he's at least five foot two. No, it's his eyes. Pale blue and go right, sort of, right through you. He's just got that distinguished, successful air about him. He's an accountant. Must be, drives a Ferrari. I bet he lives in a mansion somewhere. Oooh he's coming this way, he's coming this way...

Man 2: I'm going to kill him. No. Don't stop me. What do you mean who, that ... look over there. Tall chap with the grey hair. The policeman. Laughing like a horse there, look. He never tells the truth, he's unreliable, he's a coward and his breath smells. And he arrested me for robbing a bank. I was at home. I tell you, watching Dallas...

Man 3: She's twenty-five, she's a marvellous cook and she has a – I don't know there's something very gentle about her, very sweet. I think she's a truly good person. A lot of people forget that, of course. They only see her as a beautiful girl with a stunning figure and a lovely face. We work together, you know. She's my PA. Terrifically efficient. She's marrying the boss next week. They didn't even invite me. Yes, I would like another drink...

Woman 2: He's very dynamic and energetic. I like that in a man. Self-made man, of course. Started with nothing, and he's a millionaire now. Still only thirty-two. And he's got such good taste. I mean, look at that suit he's wearing. Double-breasted, pin stripe. So distinguished. And so modest too...

Unit 18

3.2

Jacobs:	Hello, again. And this is Pete Jacobs, Radio Headington, your local radio coming to you on 199. And this is 'Here and Now', the programme about you, with people and music. We start, this morning, with two local heroes from last night's train crash near Oxford. As you know, the 9 o'clock train was in collision with a goods train and several local people were hurt. One of the first people on the scene was Mrs Barbara Bradshaw of Derby Street, Headington, who is with us in the studio now. Good morning, Barbara.
Barbara:	Hello, Pete.
Jacobs:	Well, Barbara, tell us just what happened.
Barbara:	Well, I was walking the dog along the embankment. You know, by the railway lines, and I noticed this train. That was the goods train. It was just, er, well, you know, stationary. It was just standing there. So I didn't take much notice until this other train came along on the same line. I couldn't believe it. The driver obviously tried to slow down but there was this awful bang and he just ... the passenger train just hit the other one.
Jacobs:	And what did you do, Barbara?
Barbara:	I tied the dog up and then, sort of ran to see if I could help. I ran down the embankment.
Jacobs:	Well, as you can see, this morning's papers are calling you the heroine of the hour.
Barbara:	I don't know about that. I tried to help as many people as I could. A lot of them were hurt.
Jacobs:	You are trained in First Aid, aren't you?
Barbara:	Not really. I'm interested. There's a programme on TV about first aid, and emergencies and everything. And I just followed that. Everything sort of came back to me, from the programme.
Jacobs:	Well, the police have congratulated you for treating the injured so quickly. So it looks like you've saved some people's lives.
Barbara:	Oh! Thank you.
Jacobs:	Thank you. Let me bring in our other hero from the train crash, local man Stephen Buckley. Stephen, welcome.
Stephen:	Hello, Pete.
Jacobs:	Stephen, tell us what happened.
Stephen:	I'd just been seeing my girlfriend home, actually, Pete, and I saw the crash. I went to help. I don't know any first aid myself, so I just pulled people out of the, er, compartments, and Barbara here treated them.
Jacobs:	A lot of people were thrown clear, weren't they?
Stephen:	Yeah, that's right.
Jacobs:	Now, this is, what, the second accident we've had in the last year, and a lot of people are saying the line is dangerous. There's talk of a petition, I believe.
Stephen:	That's right, I've signed it. We want an investigation; the line made safer or something.
Jacobs:	Barbara?

Barbara: Yes, er, I didn't know there was a petition. But if I saw one I think I'd sign. Yes, yes, I agree.

Jacobs: OK. Well done again, Barbara and Stephen.

Stephen: Cheers.

Jacobs: I don't know about you, but I think they're heroes. OK. And now some more music.

Unit 19

5

Number One
(*Atonal music*)

Number Two
(*Eastern – Chinese/Japanese music*)

Number Three
(*A military march*)

Unit 20

4

Announcer: Hello and welcome to 'It's Your Line', a radio phone-in programme where you can put your views to people in the news. Today's guest is the Home Secretary, Charles Carlisle. Mr Carlisle, welcome.

Carlisle: Thank you.

Announcer: Mr Carlisle, you've been in the news recently because of your views on the crime wave. First, how serious do you think the crime wave is, and what steps will the government be taking?

Carlisle: Well, if you look at the trend since the war there is no doubt that the crime rate is going up, especially crimes against the person. We intend to be firm. We shall be increasing the maximum sentences for assault and rape. As far as the drugs problem is concerned, the number of Customs Officers will be increased and we will make every effort to catch the drug dealers.

Announcer: Thank you. Now we'll take our first call, which is from Mrs Grace Pinner from Edinburgh. Mrs Pinner, it's your line to Charles Carlisle.

Mrs Pinner: Mr Carlisle, the government's answer to crime always seems to be more force. More policemen, more Customs Officers, more pay for the police. I think if you looked at the underlying causes of crime you'd find it was unemployment, poverty...

Announcer: Yes, thank you...

Mrs Pinner: ... and the reason the kids take drugs is despair. They feel they've got no future. Now when are you going to tackle the real reasons for the crime problem?

Carlisle: Well, there has been unemployment before now. If you look at the statistics for the 1930s you will see that unemployment was actually worse, in percentage terms, but there wasn't the crime rate that we have now.

Mrs Pinner: Does that mean that the government is going to do nothing?

Carlisle: No, it doesn't. At the beginning of the programme I outlined some of the measures the government is taking, increasing the strength of police and customs and so on. We shall also be mounting a campaign of persuasion and education. There will be a poster and TV campaign about security in the home. That's the 'Lock It' campaign. Lock your doors and windows, fit security locks and so on. And you've probably already seen the television campaign showing the terrible effects of drugs.

Announcer: Thank you, Mrs Pinner. Our next caller is ... Mr Henry Jordan from Rotherham. Mr Jordan, it's your line to the Home Secretary.

Jordan: I'd like to know ... Yes, my question is whether you've given any thought to bringing, bringing back the death penalty. For serious crimes, of course. Murder and so on. I understand there have been more murders since there was no, er, since hanging was ended.

Carlisle: Well, that isn't *quite* true. I am personally against the death penalty in any form. I don't think it is a deterrent. There have been at least three cases where the wrong man was hanged and, to be honest, I think it is morally wrong. But that's a personal judgement.

Announcer: Thank you Mr Carlisle, and our next caller is ...